MW01702543

Zacharias Tanee Fomum

THE WAY OF CHISTIAN SERVICE

Éditions du Livre Chrétien
4, rue du Révérand Père Cloarec
92400 Courbevoie France
editionlivrechretien@gmail.com

First Edition, 1982, 2 500 Copies.
This book has already been produced in 5 500 Copies.
Third Edition, 2006, 2 500 Copies.

© 1990, Z. T. Fomum

All Rights Reserved

Unless otherwise stated, the Scripture quotations in this book are taken from the **New International Version of the Holy Bible,** the British Edition.

Edited:
Editions du livre chrétien
4, rue du Révérand Père Cloarec
92400 Courbevoie - FRANCE
Tél (33) 9 52 29 27 72
Email editionlivrechretien@gmail.com

Cover:
Jacques Maré

I dedicate this book to

Prisca Zei Fomum, my beloved wife and a valuable partner in my labours to know, love, and serve the Lord Jesus.

Table of Contents

Preface

This book, The Way of Christian Service, is the seventh in the Christian Way Series. The titles of the thirteen books in this series are:

Book 01	The Way of Life
Book 02	The Way of Obedience
Book 03	The Way of Discipleship
Book 04	The Way of Sanctification
Book 05	The Way of Christian Character
Book 06	The Way of Spiritual Power
Book 07	**The Way of Christian Service**
Book 08	The Way of Spiritual Warfare
Book 09	The Way of Suffering for the Lord
Book 10	The Way of Victorious Praying
Book 11	The Way of the Overcomers
Book 12	The Way of Spiritual Encouragement
Book 13	The Way of Loving the Lord

This book is about "The Way of Christian Service." Serving the Lord is something that is best begun in His immediate presence. When a person has served Him in His immediate presence and satisfied His heart, He may send such a one to go and serve on His behalf. Serving the Lord in His immediate presence consists essentially in worshipping Him. Of the leaders of the church in Antioch it was said, *"While they were worshipping the Lord and fasting, the Holy Spirit said, 'Set apart for me Barnabas and Saul for the work to which I have called them.' Then after fasting and praying, they laid their hands on them and sent them off"* (Acts 13:2-3). Barnabas and Saul were sent out to serve from the presence of the Lord to the work to which God had called them. They were ministering in His presence when He sent them away to minister on His behalf. All service of the Lord ought to begin that way.

Serving the Lord is invariably tied to resurrection life. No one can truly serve the Lord without that He, the Lord of all glory, has taken the initiative to bring that one into His service. This is so because those who serve Him must know death with Christ and resurrection with Him. Service is the flow of the life of God, and without resurrection life, there can be no flow.

People can do many things in the Lord's name, but only that which flows from life will last, and to have the flow of life there must, first of all, be death. A person will minister in proportion to the extent to which he has died and risen with Christ. Those who spare themselves the hard demands of the cross will find that they have also spared themselves the ministry of life. The extent to which a person surrenders himself to death to the world and the flesh, is the extent to which that one will know resurrection life and resurrection ministry.

There can be a work in might and power that is not fully of the Holy Spirit. Samson ministered in power, although he was out of vital fellowship with the Holy God. God demands holiness from all who would serve Him to His satisfaction.

Finally, we want to say that Christian work is acceptable in His sight and satisfies His heart only to the extent to which it is in harmony with His will and under His direction. Every work that is outside His will and direction is not only useless; it is an abomination to Him.

Too many believers today are doing nothing for the Lord. They are shy and withdrawn and lack boldness and a clear sense of direction. Where are those who would dare to step out at His command and take entire villages, towns, provinces, nations, and continents for Him? Where are those who would seek great things for Him?

My prayer is that the Lord of the harvest should use these messages to raise servants and slaves unto His glorious Son, and that such will start in His presence and, as He directs, end in the uttermost parts of the world.

Lord Jesus, ignore the weaknesses and shortcomings both of these messages and of the human messenger, and use them, Lord, for Your glory. Amen.

Zacharias Tanee Fomum,
26th October, 1982,
Yaounde, Cameroon.

CHAPTER 1

A WORK OF GOD

Before we think much about serving the Lord, I think it will be proper to define very clearly and very carefully what might rightly be called "a work of God." There is so much confusion in the world today and people are doing many things which they call "works of God." The question, however, that must be asked is, "Are these projects works of God?"

There are basically only two types of work. These are:

1. God's work.
2. The devil's work.

Anything that is not God's work is the devil's work. There is no neutral ground on which anyone can carry out a work that is neither God's nor the devil's. A work can be carried out in the name of God the Father, the Son, and the Holy Spirit which is actually the devil's work. The spiritual name by which a work is called by man does not necessarily make it a work of God.

The question then arises, "How can I distinguish God's work from the devil's? How can I be sure that in investing my life in some work I am not thereby helping the enemy to build his kingdom?"

First of all, let me say that the success of a work does not neces-sarily make it God's work. A work may appear very successful and yet not be God's. The apparent lack of success, on the other hand, does not eliminate a work from being God's work. Judged by the number of those who heard Him and continued to be faithful to Him, the work of the Lord Jesus was a failure, yet it was the very work of God.

Secondly, it is not the spiritual name by which men call a work that makes it God's work; a work may be given Biblical names and even be called after the Lord Jesus, and yet be the devil's work.

Thirdly, the motive that the workers have does not necessarily make a work God's work. The motive may be sincere and unselfish, and yet the work remains of the enemy; a pagan who sacrifices to an idol sincerely cannot, by his sincerity, transform what he is doing into God's work.

Fourthly, the degree of sacrifice involved in the work does not make it God's work. People can give themselves up to be burnt for a work which is not God's work. The sacrifice involved and the degree of consecration of the workers cannot change that which was not God's work into God's work.

Lastly, the purity of those involved in a work does not necessarily make that work a work of God; for someone may be pure but misguided or deceived.

What then are the characteristics of a work of God? Here are seven characteristics that distinguish a work of God. As you read them, prayerfully examine the work you are doing or plan to do, and see if indeed it is God's work. If you find out that it is not God's work, stop it at once; for not only have you not been working for God, but you have mistakenly and truly been helping His enemy to build that kingdom, his kingdom, that is violently opposed to the Kingdom of God.

IT MUST ORIGINATE IN GOD

All God's work must have its origin in God. He must be the Author. He must be the sole Author of it. It must be, "In the beginning God..." It must go like this:

"*And God said, >Let us make ... =* " (Genesis 1:26).

"*And God said, >Let there be light=* " (Genesis 1:3).

"*And God said, >Let there be a ...* = " (Genesis 1:6).

A work that originates in this way is heavenly in origin. All God's work is heavenly in origin. It has nothing earthly, fleshly, or devilish in it. Today people sometimes want to do something for one reason or the other. The work begins in them. They give it origin and then they call it God's work. Of course, it does not become God's work because they call it such. Of their work, they may say, "Well, I dreamt about it," or "I felt in my heart that it would be good to do this and that." They may discuss with someone who helps them to see the need to do this and that. The question remains, "Did it originate in God?" "Is God the sole Author?" I charge you before God to settle this question before Him before you continue to do even the slightest thing on the project you are involved in. You may have been hoping that it is a work of God. You may have been wishing that it be a work of God. Stop wishing and stop hoping. God does not move in the realm of human wishes and human hopes. He moves in the realm of His facts. Face them! I ask again, "Is God the sole Author of the work you are engaged in?" If He is not, then there is only one right thing that you should do, and I encourage you to do it now. It is this: Stop it immediately. You might have spent many years on it; you might have spent millions on it; many people may be involved in it with you. However, from the second that you discover that God was not the Author, you should stop it.

You cannot remedy a work that was not started by God before Him. There will be no reward whatsoever for a work that He did not give origin to. You cannot invite Him to come and take over that which He did not originate. So do not pray, saying,"Lord, You did not begin it. I began it in ignorance, but my intention was to do Your work. Come and take this work, which is the product of my sincere efforts, and make it Thine. Do it that way, Lord. Do not allow it to be wasted. Save my efforts at any cost, Lord. Be merciful to me. Look at all the effort that has been made. Look at the sacrifice. Lord, do not put it away entirely." Such praying can go on for ever, but God will never answer it. He cannot take over that which He did not start. Ultimately, what He did not start was initiated by the wicked one. Should God take over what the devil started?

There is a sense in which God is very unsparing; He could be considered wasteful. He did not spare the world when it sinned, but wiped it away with the flood. He did not spare Sodom and Gomorrah, but destroyed them. He is concerned about His work. Should He allow the enemy to be glorified and his purposes accomplished so that your puny work should stand? Never! He will never come in at a later stage to take over what He never started. It must end. It must be destroyed. If you stop it now, you will save yourself further pain. If you continue with it, it will be destroyed on that Day, and what a loss!

IT MUST FIT INTO GOD'S PURPOSE

God has an eternal purpose that was in His mind even before He laid the foundations of the world. His eternal purpose is that Christ may be all in all (Colossians 3: 11). All God's work fits into that purpose of having Christ as all in all. For anyone to call the work that he is doing God's work, it must not only originate in God, but it must also fit into God's one purpose. It must have no secondary motives.

So often today, many say that they are serving God; that they are doing God's work. Among God's twice born people, they may really have God in mind but for many of them, it is not Christ and Christ alone as the purpose. For too many, it is often Christ plus something else, such as:

1. A secret ambition to glorify self.
2. A particular doctrine.
3. A particular denomination.
4. A particular method.
5. A particular personality.
6. A particular nationality, etc.

Any work that has Christ plus something else or someone else as its goal or purpose can never be God's work. God knows no additions to Christ. For it to be God's work, it must begin in God and in God alone, and be for the glory of Christ alone.

Most human religious activities are not God's work. They have Christ plus some other goal. This becomes immediately obvious when that which is in addition to Christ is threatened. Everything will be done to protect it, and if it cannot be safely protected, the work will be abandoned, regardless of the needs of the Lord's work in that locality. This obviously shows that the main purpose was not Christ, for He is the One who is sacrificed in the crisis. Let me illustrate this point with two examples I know.

There was a shortage of Christian literature in a developing country with a young church. In talking with a visiting missionary from a big denomination with world-wide influence and finances, but which could not be registered in that country for political reasons, the big visiting missionary said, "Our denomination has a lot of evangelistic and other literature, and we have money to do a lot of things here in a short time. The problem is that we are not registered." They had the literature. They had the finances, but because the primary interest was the glory of the denomination, they could not put in much help in that needy situation because the name of their denomination would not feature prominently for many to see. They could let the interest of Christ suffer great loss. That was not a bother. The great thing was that their denomination should have pre-eminence, and since that was not forthcoming, they did nothing significant.

In another situation an international Bible-distributing organization found that for political reasons, it could not be registered as an inde-pendent body in one country. However, there was deep spiritual hunger and need in that country. There were local organizations through which the international organization could accomplish the distribution of scripture in that country, on condition that the inter-national organization dropped one of its clauses which said that it must always work as an independent body, in affiliation with no other organization. What did the visiting leaders of the international organi-zation do? They said, "We will rather close our work in this country than channel our work through the local body. Our by-laws forbid such an action." And they did! Do you see what I am saying? I am saying that although they had Christ in mind, He only occupied some small position in the whole organization. If the goal had been to serve the Lord Jesus and to serve Him alone, these people would have allowed the clause in the by-laws to falter so that that country could be reached with the Word. However, since the name of the organization and its by-laws had the central position, they won the day and Christ and His interests in that country were put aside.

As we said earlier, God knows no additions to Christ. For a work to be God's work, it must begin in God and be for Christ. If people sacrifice their lives to serve a particular doctrine, denomination, sys-tem, organization, we still ask, "Are they serving Christ and Christ alone?"

Have you ever assessed the motives behind your work? Has self-love, self-display, self-advertisement, self-will anything to do with it? If it has, then your work is mixed, and God has no use for mixtures. Mixed motives are an abomination to God. To serve God partly for His glory and partly to be noticed is idolatry. Is that how you serve? Have you ever fallen before God and said to Him, "Lord, I am an idolater. I serve You for Your glory and I serve You partly for my own glory. Have mercy on me and do a radical work in me"? Have you ever repented of the great sin of idol-worship committed by you? The idol is not a stone, or a tree, or any such thing. The idol is you!

God's work can only be done out of motives that are pure. He cannot stand mixed motives. God is pure. There is no mixture in Him whatsoever. The Lord Jesus, who is the Goal of all God's work, is pure. There is no mixture in Him whatsoever. A work that originates in God and is done for Christ must, of necessity, be pure; and no pure work can result from impure motives. This is a divine law.

IT MUST BE DONE BY GOD

The Bible says,

"*The Lord worked with them*" (Mark 16:20).

"*God created*" (Genesis 1:1).

"*God separated*" (Genesis 1:4).

"*God is at work in you ...*" (Philippians 2:13).

God cannot conceive a work for the glory of Christ and not do it Himself. Sure enough, He wants channels through which to work, but He must be the One working through such channels. The work can continue to be His only as far as He, the Author, continues to do the work through men or by the instrumentality of men.

Many treat God like an absentee Lord. They think that He had a work to be done but somehow, He went away and forgot about it. Somehow, they think that although God has abandoned the work, His initial purpose was good, and therefore, they must continue the work for Him in order to get Him out of the mess of an unaccomplished task.

Of course, it is obvious that this will not do. Anyone who thinks and acts this way thinks and acts foolishly and ignorantly, and what he does will never be a work of God.

For a work to be done by God, He must have channels through which to work. It is here that man comes in. He is God's channel, God's instrument. He works with God, but all the initiative is God's. The channel dares not tell God what to do. The channel must be totally in tune with God. When God no longer works, all the efforts of the channel will end in nothingness.

If God is to use channels, then He has the right to choose which channels to use and which ones to leave out. He is sovereign. He is under no obligation to use anyone. Anyone who is used by God knows that it is a privilege and not a right.

God somehow prefers some kinds of channels to others. We shall look into this in more detail at a later stage, but suffice it to say that if God is to use a vessel for a long time, that vessel must have some qualifications which include:

1. Purity.
2. Malleability (capacity to be beaten or twisted, into any

shape that He wants).

3. Availability.
4. Zeal.
5. Ambition.
6. Etc.

For temporary use or occasional use, He, in His sovereignty, can use anyone. He used: Samson,

Jonah,

Balaam,

Solomon,

etc.

But these were not men of deep spiritual consequence. There is a sense in which He can use anything that He chooses:

He used Balaam's ass,

He can use stones to sing, and

He can use even His enemies to accomplish His work.

In all this it will be obvious that He is the One working.

IT MUST BE DONE IN THE POWER OF THE HOLY SPIRIT

God's work must be done in the power of the Holy Spirit and in that power alone. We live in a technological age. There is nothing wrong with this, for God is the Lord of technology. The problem, however, is that technology has been made to replace the Lord. Organization has taken the place of the power of the Holy Spirit. Many evangelistic careers today would be totally grounded if the evangelists were not allowed to use the television, the radio, literature, and all the other methods of advertisement.

For many people, the fact that the invitation cards have been printed and the advertisement extensive is all they need. Sometimes there is no difference whatsoever between the way in which an evangelistic campaign is advertised and the way a boxing tournament or a pop singer is advertised. The Church not only uses worldly methods but outdoes the world in their use, and sometimes even abuses these methods.

The Lord of glory said, "*My people have committed two evils: they have forsaken me, the fountain of living waters, and hewed out cisterns for themselves, broken cisterns, that can hold no water*" (Jeremiah 2:13).

In our day, techniques, methods and shows, have been allowed to replace the Lord. Does the modern evangelistic enterprise depend absolutely on the Lord? The honest answer is "NO." The insistence today is on the training of workers, which means so many years in the Bible School, a diploma, etc. The consequence is that men with empty intellectual knowledge have replaced the prophets of God! The work is so organised to ensure that when the Holy Spirit does not move any more, it can continue as before or even better.

In a work of God, the Holy Spirit is the absolute Controller. He holds all of it together. When He moves, the work goes on. When He stops, the work stops. A work of God is linked directly to Him. He is at the very heart of it. Nothing can substitute Him.

When anyone reads the Acts of the Apostles, it is obvious that the Lord was at work by the power of the Holy Spirit. The disciples had nothing else to count on. The odds were against them. The religious authorities were against them. The political authorities were against them. Their message was unpopular. In fact, it was said of them, "*with regard to this sect we know that everywhere it is spoken against*" (Acts 28:22). Financial odds were against them. Socially, they did not have much to count on; and with regard to academic knowledge gained from schools, that, too, was in short supply among them. Yet, in spite of all these things and all these factors, there was a phenomenal work. There was no other way of accounting for it than that the Holy Spirit had worked and was working. God had said, "*Not by might, nor by power, but by my Spirit, says the Lord of Hosts*" (Zechariah 4:6).

There is human, technological, advertising, and organizational power. There is the might of human education, of money the dollar, the franc, etc. God can work without these. God's work is not bound to any of these. He can work without any of them.

There is also the power of the Holy Spirit. When that power is present, even if nothing else is, God's work will go on.

I am at a loss as to where human, technological, advertising, financial, etc, power comes in. It would have been wonderful and safe to say that if these other powers and the Holy Spirit work together, great results will be produced. However, I am not so sure of that. My own brief look at Church history does not give me the consolation needed to say that. The truth, I believe, is that the power of the Holy Spirit has often been at work to the fullest measure when other powers have been absent. These powers often come to the fullest display when the power of the Holy Spirit is least operative.

Why is this so? I think the answer lies in the channels through which God works. God created man with a capacity for single-mindedness buried into his very being. Double-mindedness is foreign to man as God meant him to be. Redeemed humanity measures closely to what was primarily in the mind of God at the beginning of creation. Therefore, redeemed men cannot truly count on the power of the Holy Spirit and on:

1. The dollar, the franc, or any other currency.
2. Organizational power.
3. Educational power.
4. Political power.
5. Denominational power.
6. All other forms of human power.

When faced with a choice between total dependence on the power of the Holy Spirit or these other powers, most people, although confessing with their lips their need and dependence on the power of the Holy Spirit, will in their inward being, depend on these other powers. This is clearly seen in the fact that the Holy Spirit will be sacrificed in order to maintain these powers.

Believers will depend absolutely on the Holy Spirit when they have nothing else to depend on. Such dependence is a prerequisite for a work of God to be done through men. These other powers are like crutches in the hands of a cripple. They enable him to do some of the things that he wants done, but they also rob him of ever walking on his own; for while they are there, they prevent him from seeing how desperate his situation is and also keep him away from the des-perate faith that hangs on God alone. It is this desperate faith that gives room for miracles.

Have you ever realized that all these other powers are broken cisterns that can hold no water? Have you ever realized that the organization of many Christian things today leaves no room for the Holy

Spirit to work, for He delights to work in freedom? Have you realized that all that you are counting on as the strength of your work:

- the superior academic training of your workers,
- the great size of your budget,
- the great number of your specialists in evangelism, pastoring, conselling, etc,
- your registration and popularity with the Caesar of the day,
- etc,

are broken cisterns that can hold no water? Do you not see that as the number and quality of these things have increased, your entire dependence on God has decreased and your willingness to compromise with the world has increased?

May I suggest that for a work of God there must be no compromise no balance between the two factors? May I suggest that there is only one way to have a work of God done, and that is by one hundred per cent dependence on the Holy Spirit and zero per cent dependence on anything else? May I suggest that all that is done by human power is totally useless for God, and worse, it opposes that which is of God, just as lshmael, the son of the flesh opposed Isaac, the son of promise and mocked him? Could it be that by your dependence on technology and all forms of human power, you have unconsciously set out to oppose God in His work, stand in His way, and frustrate His purposes? How long will you halt between the two? If human power will do, depend on it. If the power of the Holy Spirit will do, depend on it. You must, however, know that you cannot depend on both powers. Finally, remember that a work of God is that which depends on the Holy Spirit alone for its power.

IT MUST BE DONE BY MEN WHO ARE CALLED TO IT BY GOD

One thing that characterized the men of God of the Bible and the work of God that was accomplished through them was the deep certainty that God had called them to it as individuals, and, indeed, God did call them to specific tasks.

Abraham knew for certain that God had said to him, "*Go from your country and your kindred and your father's house to the land that I will show you. And I will make of you a great nation, and I will bless you, and make your name great, so that you will be a blessing*" (Genesis 12:1-2).

Moses knew for certain that there was a day when God had said to him, "*Come, I will send you to Pharaoh that you may bring forth my people, the sons of Israel, out of Egypt*" (Exodus 3: 10). All through the problems with the unwillingness of Pharaoh to let the children of Israel go out of Egypt and the difficult years in the wilderness of leading a rebellious people, that knowledge of God's personal call to that task never forsook him. He could say, even in the face of the greatest difficulties and of apparent or real failure, "The Lord called me to this work. I am not here because of my personal inclinations or because someone attracted me to it."

Joshua knew that God had said to him personally, "*...arise, go over this Jordan, you and all this people, into the land which I am giving to them, to the people of Israel*" (Joshua 1:2).

Gideon knew that the Lord had said to him clearly and distinctly, "*Go in this might of yours and deliver Israel from the hand of Midian; do not I send you?*" (Judges 6:14).

Peter knew that there was a day when the Lord Jesus had said to him, "*Do not be afraid; henceforth you will be catching men*" (Luke 5:10), and also that the Lord had said to him, "*I will give you the keys of the kingdom of heaven, and whatever you bind on earth shall be, having been bound in heaven, and whatever you loose on earth shall be, having been loosed in heaven*" (Matthew 16:19 translation).

Ananias knew for certain that the Lord had said to him, "*Rise and go to the street called Straight, and inquire in the house of Judas for a man of Tarsus named Saul; for behold, he is praying*" (Acts 9:11-12).

Paul knew for certain that the Lord had spoken to him clearly through Ananias, "*I have appeared to you for this purpose, to appoint you to serve and bear witness to the things in which you have seen me and to those in which I will appear to you, delivering you from the people and from the Gentiles to whom I send you to open their eyes, that they may turn from darkness to light and from the power of Satan to God, that they may receive forgiveness*" (Acts 26:16-18).

For all these men, and for multitudes of others, there was that personal element of a deep personal transaction between them and God about the call of God upon their lives. For each one of them, there was that, "I" on God's part and "You" on the part of the vessel to be used. It was intimate. It was certain.

They each received a personal call from the Lord. They were not in God's work, because:

- they wanted to display some special abilities,
- they were jobless and, therefore, wanted some form of employment,
- they wanted a name for themselves,
- they had seen others accomplish similar feats and they wanted to imitate them in God's name, or because
- they saw some need and decided to do something about it.

They were there because God wanted them there and had called them to it.

Today in the Body of Christ, there is much that is done out of:

- party spirit,
- imitation,
- worldly demands and trends,
- etc.

No such work is God's work. It may appear successful; it may appear spiritual; it may seem to serve the interest of God, but ultimately it will be shown for what it is. The Lord Jesus said, "*Every plant which my heavenly Father has not planted will be rooted up*" (Matthew 15:13).

The question arises, "What if God intends to have a work done and the wrong people take up the task and begin to do it out of relationship with Him and without His clear instructions? Will it remain His work?" It will not! It cannot! It only remains God's work when it is being done by people who are called to it by God Himself. Take, for example, the work done by the first apostles. This team was not comprised of men who had applied to work for the Lord. The Bible says, "*And he went up on the mountain, and called to him those whom he desired; and they came to him. And he appointed twelve ...*" (Mark 3:13-14).

He called to Himself those whom He desired and out of those whom He desired He appointed twelve. So there was:

1. The world.
2. The multitude out of the world that came often to hear Him.
3. Those whom He desired out of the multitude and therefore

called to the mountain.

4. The twelve whom he appointed out of those whom He desired. To these twelve He gave special privileges:

- to be with Him as the others could not be,
- to be sent out to preach, and
- to have authority over demons.

Only people called so clearly by the Lord can do His work.

Permit me to repeat that God is sovereign in His choice of men. Sometimes He uses worthless men, heathens, rebels, etc, to accomplish His short-term plans. The glory is His and not that of the person used. For a deep and lasting work, He calls to it people who can co-operate with Him. Such people know Him, feel after Him, obey Him, are pure in every way, thus resembling the Lord Jesus. It is the work done by such men that truly satisfies the heart of God. They do the business that is closest to the heart of God.

It is not, therefore, just a matter of being used by God. I may not bother too much about whom I use to clear the grass around my compound, but if I want someone to carry out a heart operation on my son, I will carefully scrutinise the qualifications of the people available and will appoint only the best to do it. If I do not find a suitable person, I will wait for some time rather than entrust my son into the hands of just anyone, for I do not only want an operation but a successful operation.

There are thus works of God that can be compared to the clearing of grass around a compound, which He can allow anyone to do. There are other things to be done, "The work of God," which in the deepest sense of the word can be compared to heart operations. To these He calls only people who are truly qualified; for only they can handle such jobs.

Do you then see why a nation can go for hundreds of years without much happening until He finds a man who qualifies for use in a special way? He waits for those who find in Him the satisfaction of their hearts and who can satisfy His heart.

IT MUST BE DONE BY GOD'S METHODS

Does it matter to God how things are done? Is it not enough that His work is done? Does the end not justify the means? Must someone who is interested in the Lord's work not just look for methods that work, irrespective of the author of the methods? Is it not enough that the Gospel is proclaimed irrespective of how it is done? Even if the wrong methods are used, does the conversion of people to the Lord not make one forget the methods and just thank God that souls are being won into His Kingdom? These are serious questions and we must face them squarely.

When God wanted the tabernacle constructed, He said to Moses, "*According to all that I show you concerning the pattern of the tabernacle, and of all its furniture, so shall you make it*" (Exodus 25:9). He further said, "*And you shall make a lampstand of pure gold. The base and the shaft of the lampstand shall be made of hammered work; its cups, its capitals, and its flowers shall be of one piece with it; and there shall be six branches going out of its sides, three branches of the lampstand out of one side of it and three branches of the lampstand out of the other side of it; three cups made like almonds, each with capital and flower, one branch, and three cups made like almonds, each with capital and flower, on the other branch so for the six branches going out of the lampstand; and on the lampstand itself four cups made like almonds, with their capitals and flowers, and a capital of one piece with it under each pair of the six branches going out from the lampstand. Their capitals and their branches shall be of one piece with it, the whole of it one piece of hammered work of pure gold. And you shall make the seven lamps for it; and the lamps shall be set up so as to give light upon the space in front of it. Its snuffers and their trays shall be of pure gold. Of a talent of pure gold shall it be made, with all these utensils. And see that you make them after the pattern for them, which is being shown you on the mountain*" (Exodus 25:31-40).

God did not just ask that the lampstand should be made and then leave it to Moses to decide with what material it was to be constructed. He specified the material pure gold and then He went on to excruciating details on how it was to be done. He did not only do this with the lampstand. He did it also for the ark, the table, the tabernacle, the veil, the altar, and the court of the tabernacle. Everything was to be done according to well-defined, God-given details. There was no room for the ideas and the opinions of Moses. All had to be God's ideas from start to finish.

This did not apply only to the tabernacle. The garments of the priests and the services in the tabernacle had to be carried out in God's way in every detail. God had a heavenly model, Moses saw it and all that he was constructing on earth had to conform in every detail to the heavenly model.

It was imperative for Moses to see the heavenly model; for God was constantly saying, "*See that you make them after the pattern for them, which is being shown you on the mountain*" (Exodus 25:40). "*And you shall erect the tabernacle according to the plan for it which has been shown you on the mountain*" (Exodus 26:30). "*You shall make it hollow, with boards; as it has been shown you on the mountain, so shall it be made*" (Exodus 27:8). It also made it absolutely necessary for Moses to construct according to the details that he had seen. He was not to construct without seeing, and he was not to leave out any detail that he had seen or incorporate into it some detail, however small, that he had not seen.

As far as the work that God wanted Moses to do was concerned, the following were clear:

1. God had a heavenly model.

2. God showed Moses the heavenly model.

3. Moses was expected to see the heavenly model clearly.

4. Moses took time to see the heavenly model well.

5. Moses had to build the earthly tabernacle so that it conformed in every way and in every detail to the heavenly model.

6. God was not only concerned about the overall structure, He was concerned about each detail.

7. Each detail had something special to do with the will of God, and its absence would have introduced something horrible into God's design.

8. Moses had no right whatsoever to introduce any thought or opinion of his into the construction.

9. Moses, as the leader and earthly architect, had the responsibility of communicating to all who were to be involved with him what the heavenly model was like, and he had to ensure that they, too, saw clearly what the model was like; he had to ensure that they, too, saw clearly what the model was.

10. Moses had to ensure that the people built according to that model. He had to insist on each detail. The people's personal opinions about the model were not important. In fact, their opinions were to be excluded completely. What the pagan nations around thought of the model, or how they were doing their own things was not to be considered at all. They were to follow God's instructions and it was expected that because they loved the Lord, they would

love His model. However, even if they did not love His model, they were to build according to it, because it was His work and not theirs.

11. The difficulty in securing the right materials was not to deter them from doing the work or allow them to make do with what was available.

12. Only people who saw what that model was and were prepared to surrender unconditionally to constructing after that model and at any cost to themselves were allowed on the job.

This way of having God's work done was not limited to Moses. The Lord of all glory, in sending out the twelve on a missionary journey, gave them very precise instructions as to where they were to go and where they were not to go. He also gave them the message they were to preach and what their activities were to be. He gave them financial instructions, and also instructions about food and clothing. He also gave them details about their relationship with the public. He said to them, "*Go nowhere among the Gentiles, and enter no town of the Samaritans, but go rather to the lost sheep of the house of Israel. And preach as you go, saying, 'The kingdom of heaven is at hand.' Heal the sick, raise the dead, cleanse lepers, cast out demons. You received without paying, give without pay. Take no gold, nor silver, nor copper in your belts, no bag for your journey, nor two tunics, nor sandals, nor a staff; for the labourer deserves his food. And whatever town or village you enter, find out who is worthy in it, and stay with him until you depart. As you enter the house, salute it. And if the house is worthy, let your peace come upon it; but if it is not worthy, let your peace return to you. And if any one will not receive you or listen to your words, shake off the dust from your feet as you leave that house or town. Truly, I say to you, it shall be more tolerable on the day of judgement for the land of Sodom and Gomorrah than for that town*" (Matthew 10:5-15).

Jesus did not only give specific and detailed instructions to the twelve. He also gave specific and detailed instructions to the seventy whom He also sent out. The instructions were similar to those given to the twelve, but different. He said to them, "*The harvest is plentiful, but the labourers are few; pray therefore the Lord of the harvest to send out labourers into his harvest. Go your way; behold, I send you out as lambs in the midst of wolves. Carry no purse, no bag, no sandals; and salute no one on the road. Whatever house you enter, first say, 'Peace be to this house!'; and if a son of peace is there, your peace shall rest upon him, but if not, it shall return to you. And remain in the same house, eating and drinking what they provide, for the labourer deserves his wages; do not go from house to house. Whenever you enter a town and they receive you, eat what is set before you; heal the sick in it and say to them, 'The kingdom of God has come near to you.' But whenever you enter a town and they do not receive you, go into its streets and say, 'Even the dust of your town that clings to our feet, we wipe off against you; nevertheless know this, that the kingdom of God has come near.' I tell you, it shall be more tolerable on that day for Sodom than for that town*" (Luke 10:2-12).

We shall come back to this theme of God's model, God's detailed instructions and working according to them later on. It suffices for the moment to say that there is a model in the mind of God for every work that He wants done. All who are called by Him to lead must see that model and build according to it. They must also ensure that they communicate what they have seen to those who are to work alongside with them. They must refuse and actively resist any attempts to allow their own thoughts, opinions, wishes, etc, to come in. They must also resist all attempts by the world to influence them. In this way, the work will be a heavenly one, God's work.

This means that the methods used must be God's own and not those that are borrowed from the popular film stars, night club managers, or the great money magnates of the day. The methods, like the work, will have to be received from the Lord and adhered to until He gives further instructions. Such methods will very often be contrary to the world's methods, and at times look very foolish, but they will do God's work and accomplish results that will satisfy the heart of God. So, if a work is meant to satisfy the world, methods that the world finds satisfactory should be used, but if the goal is to satisfy the heart of God, His methods must be used.

If a clear-thinking man examines what goes on today in the name of popular evangelism, preaching, teaching, church-planting, Christian publishing business, etc, it is obvious that the whole thing has been patterned after the world, and that, to some extent, the Christian seems to envy the world for having such success-producing methods. Somehow, in many organisations, even in those where decision making is in the hands of believers, the methods that are used seem to say that God's methods don't work. Take the book of the Acts of the Apostles and write out the evangelistic and missionary strategy and methods in it and put them side by side with the methods and strategy of the popular evangelists and denominations of today and you will immediately see the difference. In the book of Acts, God's methods were used and God-ordained results were obtained. Today human and worldly methods are used and, no wonder, the church stands impotent before a watching world.

When God's methods were used, He had to be at the centre of the work and not at the periphery; He had to be all in all or else all would fail completely. When human methods are used, man has to be at the centre, or else all will fail. Man, being at the centre of them, has to manipulate this and that, and compromise here and there so that things might work.

The question is, "Can a work that originates in God and is done by the people of His choosing, yet being carried out by methods that are not His, continue to have His full backing?" About this, two things can be said.

First of all, if God commits His work to the right persons, such people are likely to seek His methods and use them. Secondly, if such people begin with His methods but allow themselves to be carried away by the world, the work may continue, but God will withdraw from the centre of it. He may still allow some blessings upon it, but just as He allows sunshine and rain on the wicked, but the blessings are not an indication of His approval.

IT MUST BE DONE IN GOD'S TIMING

God is not only concerned that His work be done by His methods, with Him as its Originator and with Christ as its purpose, but He is also concerned that it be done in His own timing. He has His time for all His work. The Bible says, "*But when the time had fully come God sent forth his Son, born of woman, born under the law, to redeem those who were under the law*" (Galatians 4:4). "*For he has made known to us in all wisdom and insight the mystery of his will, according to his purpose which he set forth in Christ as a plan for the fullness of time, to unite all things in him, things in heaven and things on earth*" (Ephesians 1:9-10). Man sinned thousands of years earlier. God had a plan worked out to redeem fallen man, but He did not rush. He waited for His own time the fullness of time to bring to pass His mighty purposes in salvation. All God's actions are on exact time. He is never in a hurry, He is never too early, and He is never too late.

The Lord Jesus was deeply concerned that things should be done at the time that God had set for them. At the beginning of His ministry He said to Mary His mother, "*O woman, what have you to do with me? My hour has not yet come*" (John 2:4). To His brothers He said, "*My time has not yet come, but your time is always here. The world cannot hate you, but it hates me because I testify of it that its works are evil. Go to the feast yourselves; I am not going up to the feast, for my time has not yet fully come. So saying, He remained in Galilee. But after His brothers had gone up to the feast, then he also went up, not publicly but in private*" (John 7:6-10).

In this passage, we see something of the Lord Jesus concept of time. There was the feast in Jerusalem. He was to go to it. His brothers wanted to precipitate His going. They were working in the general realm of things. The general indications of time showed that it was about time. They decided that it was time to act and so encouraged the Lord to do so. The Lord, however, distinguished between their time and His time. Their time was already there. It was general and it was dictated by outward events. His own time was not yet there. It was dictated to His spirit by the Holy Spirit, and was independent of what happened outwardly. They moved as outward circumstances indicated and went up to the feast. He waited for the Holy Spirit to dictate the time, and when it was fully come, the Holy Spirit said to His spirit, "It is time now for you to go to the feast. However, do not go publicly. Go privately." And off He went and He was on time.

Again at that very feast, Jesus knew when to say what. It was, "*On the last day of the feast, the great day, Jesus stood up and proclaimed, 'If any one thirst, let him come to me and drink'* " (John 7:37). Such a proclamation would have been out of place on the first day. It would also have been out of place on the last but one day. However, He waited until the right day.

So God's work must be done in His time. No one can move ahead of God and yet do His work, nor can someone lag behind Him and still do His work. There is danger in rushing ahead of Him. There is also danger in lagging behind Him. People can rush ahead out of carnal anxiety and worldly pressure. Also, others can, out of fear and doubt, hesitate, check this thing and that thing, consult this person and that person, etc, and fail God by missing His time.

When the Lord Jesus heard that Lazarus was dead, He did not hurriedly rush to Bethany. He waited, continuing with His normal ministry. He arrived at Bethany four days "late" but was on God's time to raise Lazarus from the dead. He was neither early nor late. He said, "*Are there not twelve hours in the day? If any one walks in the day, he does not stumble, because he sees the light of this world. But if any one walks in the night, he stumbles, because the light is not in him*" John 11:9-10). So we can illustrate it this way:

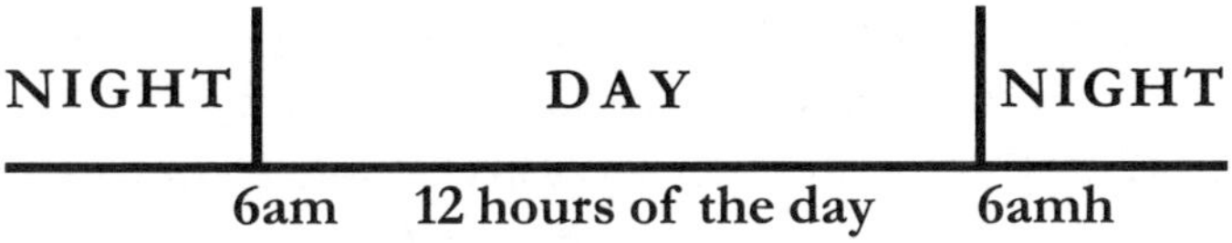

Those who work before 6:00 a.m. work in darkness. They have rushed ahead. Those who work after 6.00 p.m. work in the dark. They have lagged behind.

Someone may ask, "Why is it so important to do God's work in God's time?" To this I offer a number of reasons: First of all, that is when God wants His work done. He must be obeyed. Secondly, God has so programmed how His things should go. It is like the railway programme of a big country with millions of railways and billions of trains. Everything is programmed so that train A will be at station Z at a particular minute. In order to do that, it must leave station Y at a fixed time and go at a fixed speed. Train B has also been scheduled to be at X at a fixed time. If train A is late and train B is on time, there will be a crash at some point because the two trains were never meant to cross at the time at which they now cross. A similar problem will arise if train A started earlier than scheduled. It, too, would cause a crash by doing that.

Do you then see why timing is important for God's work to be done? Do you see that this raises another important factor about

God's work which we have not yet considered? This has to do with the speed factor. Train A could start off on time, but if it is too slow or too fast, it would cause the same problems as those caused by starting off too late or too early.

Therefore, in God's work, it is not only important to be doing God's work in His time, but it must also be done at the speed at which God wants it done. No one dares be satisfied by the fact that he is serving the Lord. He must serve the Lord at the speed that God wants. If, for example, He wants twenty souls won every day, men may congratulate the one who wins ten, fifteen or nineteen, but no such person will receive the congratulations of the Lord. God's twenty remains twenty, and those who want to satisfy Him must work in such fellowship with Him that they will win the desired twenty.

This also means that anyone who permits anything to come between the Lord and himself, even a small matter that may affect God's work negatively, even if only to a small extent, becomes a serious problem to God. Such a one who hinders in a small way becomes ultimately just as bad as the one who hinders in a big way. This should make all of God's servants stop and rethink.

CHAPTER 2

A DISTINCTIVE MINISTRY

There are many activities that fall into the group of what may be called, "General Ministry." Such activities include things like:

- General giving to the Lord,
- General praying,
- General evangelism.

To all such activities all the children of the Lord are called, and no further revelation is needed in order that such work be done. No believer should wait for further revelation before he joins the rest of the church in carrying out such ministry. All should join in without further questions.

However, there can be a special ministry to which the Lord calls people as individuals or as groups of individuals. To such ministry the Lord says: "You, brother so and so, I want you to carry out the following work for me. "When God gives a particular work to a particular individual or a particular group of individuals, there you have a distinctive ministry.

REVELATION: A PREREQUISITE FOR DISTINCTIVE MINISTRY

Revelation is a prerequisite for ministry. A distinctive ministry depends on a distinctive revelation from the Lord. For such revelation, there has to be:

A Given Situation

In Exodus 1:8-14, the Bible says, "*Now there arose a new king over*

Egypt, who did not know Joseph. And he said to his people, Behold, the people of Israel are too many and too mighty for us. Come, let us deal shrewdly with them, lest they multiply, and, if war befall us, they join our enemies and fight against us and escape from the land. Therefore, they set taskmasters over them to afflict them with heavy burdens; and they built for Pharaoh store-cities, Pithom and Raamses. But the more they were oppressed, the more they multiplied and the more they spread abroad. And the Egyptians were in dread of the people of Israel. So they made the people of Israël serve with rigour, and made their lives bitter with hard service, in mortar and brick, and in all kinds of work in the field; in all their work they made them serve with rigour."

In the course of those many days the king of Egypt died. And the people of Israel groaned under their bondage, and cried out for help, and their cry under bondage came up to God (Exodus 2: 23).

This was a given situation, a specific situation. There was a suffering people who were in such a great need that something specific had to be done for them. That is the first prerequisite for special ministry.

God Must Become One with the Given Situation

A situation may exist and be quite terrible. However, if God does not become one with it by identifying Himself with it, no one can carry out a special ministry in that situation and yet satisfy the heart of God. So, a distinctive ministry is not just a personal response to a necessary situation. It is not a person looking around and saying to himself, "There is need here. What can I do about it? I will do this and that and, hopefully, God will bless my efforts."

The children of Israel were suffering in bondage. That could have gone on for hundreds of years without God identifying Himself with their situation. He would then have done nothing for them.

However, God did become one with the given situation. How did He become one with that situation? He said, "*I have seen the affliction of my people who are in Egypt, and have heard their cry because of their taskmasters; I know their sufferings*" (Exodus 3:7). God saw, heard, and knew their suffering.

God must see the situation in a special, distinctive way. He must hear the cry in a distinctive way, and He must decide to know their suffering in a distinctive way. We insist that God must be fully involved. He was involved with the Christ on the cross. The Bible says, "in Christ God was reconciling the world to himself@ (2 Corinthians 5:19). He was not aloof. He is not aloof. His being suffers as His people suffer. Do you know that there can be no groan or tear or heartache for the cause of the Gospel without which God groans, sheds tears, and has heartaches twice as much? The Lord of heaven is involved. He is the God who feels with His people. No one can effectively carry out a distinctive ministry and by so doing satisfy the heart of God, if God was not totally involved with the pain and the agony of the people. Is that perhaps the reason why so much that passes for ministry today does not satisfy the heart of God?

God Must Decide to Do Something about the Situation

The Lord, having seen the situation and having become one with it, decided to do something about it. He said, "*I have come down to deliver them out of the hand of the Egyptians, and to bring them up out of that land to a good and broad land, a land flowing with milk and honey*" (Exodus 3:8).

God said, "I have come down." Eternal Glory came down to meet a human need. God is involved. He comes down and takes the move to do something about totally hopeless and helpless situations. He said He had come down to accomplish three things:

1 - to deliver them out of the hand of the Egyptians,

2 - to bring them out of that land.

3 - to bring them to a good and broad land flowing with milk and honey.

God had three goals in mind as His answer for the given situation. The distinctive ministry involved in that situation had to do with accomplishing part or all of those goals. Having set those goals and having come down to accomplish them, it was impossible that He should fail to do so. God never changes His mind about His purposes. He goes right ahead, regardless of opposition from the wicked one, and does that which He sets out to do.

God Must Decide the Time When He Wants It Done

God, having decided to do something about the situation, had to face the matter of time. When must it be done? We have already discussed this at length in our study of what constitutes a work of God. We shall only add a few brief comments here. God said: "*And now . . .*" (Exodus 3:9). God had been hearing their cry long before, but at a particular point in time, His time was fully come and when He heard their cry this time, He decided to do something about it at once. God waited for that time. Even in Gospel business, this matter of God's time, God's right time, the fullness of God's time, is of utmost importance. If a person is forced to make a premature commitment to the Lord Jesus, it may lead to a premature spiritual baby, and most of them die or are sickly all their spiritual lives. On the other hand, we know that too much delay can lead to a still-birth. We know of people who died without making the right commitment to the Saviour because they kept pushing the decision into the future until it was too late. God always acts on time. He is never late.

God Appoints a Person through Whom to Carry Out His Purpose

When God's time fully comes, He appoints a person through whom He will work. God's appointments are according to His eternal purpose. God's eternal purpose is that there might be a Body, a bride for His eternal Son a Body that conforms to the Head. So, all of God's purposes relate ultimately to the Church. His appointments are not emergency operations. About Jeremiah He said, "*Before I formed you in the womb I knew you, and before you were born I consecrated you; I appointed you a prophet to the nations*" (Jeremiah 1:5). About Isaiah it was said, "*The Lord called me from the womb, from the body of my mother he named my name*" (Isaiah 49:1). Paul said, "*But when he who had set me apart before I was born and had called me through his grace was pleased to reveal his Son to me*" (Galatians 1: 15).

So God called each of these people individually. He also called them to specific ministries. Jeremiah was appointed a prophet to the nations and given clear specifications about his ministry. The Lord said to him, "*Do not say, 'I am only a youth,' for to all to whom I send you, you shall go, and whatever I command you, you shall speak. Be not afraid of them for I am with you to deliver you. Then the Lord put forth his hand and touched my mouth and the Lord said to me, "Behold, I have put my words in your mouth. See, I have set you this day over nations and over kingdoms, to pluck up and to break down, to destroy and to overthrow, to build and to plant*" (Jeremiah 1:9-10).

Isaiah was appointed and commissioned. The Bible says: "*He made my mouth like a sharp sword, in the shadow of his hand he hid me; he made me a polished arrow, in his quiver he hid me away* " (Isaiah 49:2).

Paul was appointed and told: "*I have appeared to you for this purpose, to appoint you to serve and bear witness to the things in which you have seen me and to those in which I will appear to you, delivering you from the people and from the GentilesC to whom I send you to open their eyes, that they may turn from darkness to light and from the power of Satan to God, that they may receive forgiveness of sins and a place among those who are sanctified by faith in me*" (Acts 26:16-18).

God appointed each of these to a specific ministry right before they were born. Of course, if they had failed Him, He would have cast them away, but by His grace they did not fail Him.

Before you became a biological reality in your mother's womb, God already had a particular ministry prepared for you. This is God's perfect will for you.

God Reveals Himself to the One Appointed

When God appoints a person to carry out a certain distinctive ministry, the first thing that He does is not to give that ministry to the person. That one must know God. He must have God revealed to him at the personal level. Not until God has been thus revealed to him can God reveal the ministry to which He is calling him. We insist that this personal revelation of God must precede the revelation of ministry. There are, unfortunately, those who think that they have been sent out by a God they do not know to carry out some special work for Him. This is total folly.

Paul said : "When it pleased Him to reveal His Son to me in order that I might preach him among the Gentiles..." First of all, a revelation of the Son to him; and secondly, his preaching Him among the Gen-tiles.

The twelve apostles were called to be with Him so that they might know Him; and only secondarily, to be sent out to preach, heal, and deliver (Mark 3:14-15). The seven sons of Sceva did not know Him, but they tried to minister in His name and incurred upon themselves the wrath of demons to whom they were not equal (Acts 19:13-17).

Moses was God's chosen vessel for the deliverance of Israel out of the hand of the Egyptians, out of Egypt and their transfer into the Promised Land. We shall look at the call of God on him, the revelation of God to him and the commissioning of him by the Lord in some detail.

THE CALL OF MOSES

What was Moses before that history-changing day when he personally received the call of God? The Bible tells us that the hand of God was at work already in his life preparing him for the ministry that God had prepared for him right from the foundations of the world.

First of all, God miraculously spared him when other Hebrew boys were being killed. "*By faith Moses, when he was born, was hid for three months by his parents, because they saw that the child was beautiful and they were not afraid of the king's edict*" (Hebrews 11:23). So God overruled that Moses should not be killed. There is a sense in which it is obvious that he could not be killed because God had a mighty purpose worked out for him from the foundations of the world, and that purpose could not be thwarted (Job 42:2).

God arranged for Moses to have all the best natural advantages that were possible to have in those days, by arranging for him to be brought up as the son of Pharaoh's daughter. He thus had the best of everything that Egypt (representing the world) could offer. The

Bible says, "*And Moses was instructed in all the wisdom of the Egyptians*" (Acts 7:22). He continued in the court of Pharaoh until he was forty years old and "*he was mighty in his words and deeds*" (Acts 7:22). So it was not a fool that God called to carry out that mighty and far-reaching ministry. It was a man who, had he chosen the world, could have had almost everything in it. Many think that God wants people who cannot do anything else to come and serve Him. This is very far from the truth.

A young man once wrote to this writer, saying: "I have tried many things and they have not worked. At the moment my business as a carpenter is failing. I think the best thing for me to do is to go to Bible School. Would you kindly recommend me?"

He received the following reply: "If you cannot get wood to obey you, you will find it even more difficult to get hardened sinners to obey you into the new life."

Do you see the point I am making? Many think that when a man cannot do anything else, he should become a preacher of the Gospel full-time, so that the churches should help him to earn some bread which he could not successfully earn in the world. The sad thing is that there are people, and I fear, many people, in the "full-time ministry" who are there because they could not do anything else. They are there to stand in the way of the churches of God! God must have the best of the world to serve Him. Paul to whom God gave another very far-reaching ministry (he wrote over half of all the books in the New Testament) as well schooled in the learning that is of this world. Even fishermen like Peter and the others, were successful fishermen. They were not stranded men who saw in following Jesus an opportunity to make a living. In a worldly sense, following the Lord Jesus did not advance them. They gained nothing worldly from it.

God knew that Moses had these advantages and he (Moses) knew that he had them. God also knew that if Moses was called at that time, he would depend on his natural abilities and not on God, or he would depend partly on God and partly on his abilities. In order to ensure that Moses, though having all these abilities, would rely solely on Him for the task to which he would be called, the Lord allowed him to go through forty years in which he was humbled, and as Dr. Joe Church put it to us one day in Uganda, "He who had thought that he was somebody learned that he was nobody." God humbled him. He had tried to deliver the children of Israel through carnal means, but God arranged for him to be discovered. He fled from Egypt. Before fleeing from Egypt, he made a far-reaching choice. He could have continued as Pharaoh's daughter's son and possible heir to the Egyptian throne, but he did not do so. The Bible says, "*By faith Moses, when he was grown up, refused to be called the son of Pharaoh's daughter, choosing rather to share ill-treatment with the people of God than to enjoy the fleeting pleasures of sin. He consid-ered abuse suffered for the Christ greater wealth than the treasures of Egypt, for he looked forward to the reward*" (Hebrews 11-24-26).

All who would be called to distinctive ministry by the Lord will sooner or later go through the same experience that Moses went through; for, in a sense, their call and appointment to special ministry is conditioned upon their complying with God's conditions.

1. Moses refused to be called the son of Pharaoh's daughter. All his earthly glory was tied to this and he refused it. All would-be servants of the Lord have something to refuse.

2. Moses chose rather to share ill-treatment with the people of God than to enjoy the fleeting pleasures of sin. He made a choice and that choice was in the direction of suffering and identification with the unpopular people of God. He made a choice against the fleeting pleasures of sin, of worldliness, position, worldly security,

etc. Have your eyes been opened to see the world and all that it offers as fleeting and sinful? I do not say that fame, honour, riches, etc are not pleasurable, but I ask, have you seen them for what they are? Do you know that they will not last? Have you made the choice? What have you chosen?

3. Moses considered abuse suffered for Christ greater than the treasures of Egypt. It is as if Moses put things on the balance. On the one side was the abuse suffered for Christ, and on the other side were the treasures of Egypt. On the balance in Moses' heart then, the treasures of Egypt had some weight, but the abuse suffered for Christ weighed more and he chose what weighed more the abuse suffered for Christ. The apostle Paul faced a similar situation; he too had a balance in his heart. On one side was the surpassing knowledge of Jesus Christ his Lord, and on the other side was all that he ever had, all that he had, and all that he would ever have. It, in fact, included all the world together and all that is in it. The surpassing worth of knowing Christ did not only weigh more, the world and all that it offered were terribly offensive to him by comparison. He put it this way: "*But whatever gain I had, I counted as loss for the sake of Christ. Indeed I count everything as loss because of the surpassing worth of knowing Christ Jesus my Lord. For his sake I have suffered the loss of all things, and count them as refuse, in order that I may gain Christ*" (Philippians 3:7-8). What of the balance in your heart? Have you considered it?

4. Moses had the courage to leave Egypt. He was not afraid of the king. Those who fear men cannot fear God and those who fear God are free from the fear of men. All who would be given a specific ministry by the Lord must have the courage to go against the tide of public opinion, the tide of the opinion of religious leaders, the tide of political opinion, and the tide of principalities and powers. No coward can go far with God while keeping his cowardice. The early apostles told the religious leaders of the day, "*We*

must obey God rather than men" (Acts 5:29). I am not saying that men should not be obeyed. There are circumstances under which it is possible to obey God and obey men. This must be done. However, if men demand that they be obeyed and God be disobeyed, all who will go far with God will certainly choose to obey God.

So, Moses thus left these things and made these choices. He then entered God's School of Humiliation. He was in that school for forty years. It is one of the most important schools in the University of God. It is a school where the subject matter is not so easily incorporated into the being of the student. It is a school where the theoretical knowledge does not help very much. People can acquire a lot of theoretical knowledge from some Bible School or seminary over a period of two or three years; and in many ways such knowledge, mentally acquired but not incorporated into character and transformed into life, causes carnal people to think that they know God, and even gives carnal men lordship over the people of God. It is needless to say that God does not appoint such men into office. One of God's servants said, "A good sermon takes ten years to prepare. A better one takes twenty years." I want to suggest that these good sermons are prepared in the School of Humiliation. In that school, God teaches the theoretical part of the course in a very short time, but because He is not out for theoretical knowledge but for character and life, He leaves the student there for a long time. Forty years was a long time, but it was necessary. Had it required less time for Moses to graduate from that school, God would not have kept him there for all that time.

One important thing about the schools in the University of God is that all the students have to enroll in all basic schools. They cannot specialize until all the courses in the basic schools have been passed. He does not promote failures. He cannot be bribed. He accepts no excuses. You may ask me what I consider to be the foremost of the basic schools in the University of God. I consider the following schools as absolutely essential:

1. The School of Love of God: The Father, the Son, and the Holy Spirit, and people.
2. The School of Suffering.
3. The School of Humiliation.

These to me are the three most basic schools. Then you can have:

4. The School of Peace.
5. The School of Patience.
6. The School of joy.
7. The School of Kindness.
8. The School of Goodness.
9. The School of Faithfulness.

There are other important schools, including:

10. The School of Holiness.
11. The School of Spiritual power.
12. The School of Discipleship.
13. The School of Overcoming.
14. The School of Prayer.

Then there is another school, the School of Service, in which courses like the following are taught:

1. Waiting on God.
2. Evangelism.

3. Pastoring.
4. Teaching.
5. Church Planting.
6. Church administration.

God never admits anyone to the three fundamental schools who does not have the entry qualification. This is the degree B.A. (born again, born from above; born of the Holy Spirit). This initial degree is awarded by the University of God Entrance Department to all who repent of their sins and receive Jesus Christ as their Lord and Saviour. With God's B.A., a person must enroll in the School of Fundamental Studies and take lessons in love, suffering, and humiliation. He can carry out studies in other schools fundamentally, but real progress is measured by the progress in those three schools. Some prefer to start in the School of Power and from there jump to the School of Service and enroll in Evangelism, while skipping the course on "Waiting on God. " Such moves are not permitted by the academic registrar of the University of Heaven and director of the School of Service, the Holy Spirit. People who deceive themselves with that type of programme and continue to reject the other schools may find that the Chancellor of that University God the Father will not sign their diplomas. They will, as such, not be given any distinctive ministry by Him, although they have freedom to go and make noise all over the world about their ministry and even produce some results.

After forty years in the School of Humiliation, in which he also took courses in some of the other schools, Moses was now prepared to have God reveal Himself to him and then give him his foreordained ministry.

Do you see why the children of Israel had to remain in bondage for so long? Their deliverer was still in school, and God had to wait for him to complete the basic courses.

Is there a situation in which you are wondering why God does not act? Do you sometimes wonder if God is deaf to your prayers that are definitely according to His revealed will? The answer is partly that He has chosen to co-work with men. He has decided to have men as His co-workers, and so until the chosen man is ready, He is more or less forced to act as if He did not care, although He cares very much. Would you be patient? Could it also be that He has not acted because you are in the School of Patience and the thing about which you want Him to act quickly is just the lesson He is teaching you at the moment in that school? Do not fight. Wait. Learn your lesson. Help Him to act faster by learning your lesson quickly.

Coming back to Moses, can you imagine the difference in position between his former state as a prince of Egypt and his present one as a shepherd? Yet, his training in the School of Humiliation was not wasted, for he learned to lead the flock and later on he was to lead people.

Then he came to Horeb, to the mountain of God. There he saw a burning bush that was not consumed. He was very close to the point of contact with God. He saw the burning bush and he wanted to know more. There must have been a desire in his heart to know the God of his people.

God saw that he turned aside to see, and God called out to him from the burning bush, "Moses, Moses!" It was a two-fold call. God was saying:

1. Moses, know Me.
2. Moses, go out for Me.

God's call is always a two-fold call. Moses answered and the deed was done. God had called and Moses had responded. From that time on, Moses belonged to God in a special way.

God always speaks out. He always calls out. Many people do not hear Him because they are too busy talking to Him. They are too busy with their monologues.

THE INESCAPABLE HOLINESS

Immediately after Moses responded to the call of God, he was faced with the holiness of God. He could not come near as he was. He removed his shoes; for he was on holy ground. God would not reveal Himself further to Moses until the question of holiness was settled. He would also not reveal the distinctive ministry that He had for Moses until this thing was settled.

Permit me to talk to you at the personal level. Is there some known sin in your life known but not confessed and not forsaken? If that is the case, God will not reveal Himself to you any further, and He will not reveal to you the distinctive ministry that He has in store for you. Are you involved in some questionable practice? Are you involved in a questionable relationship? Is there some cloud between you and God? It may only be a small issue. It may cut God off only a bit, but as long as you know that it is there and you do not do something at once to put things right, God will not reveal Himself to you any further, and He will not reveal the distinctive ministry that He has in store for you.

Do you see how serious the whole matter of total separation from sin and the putting on of Christ is? We said earlier that all distinctive ministry was conditioned on revelation and revelation is conditioned on holiness. Therefore, the person who continues in sin has forfeited his privilege of knowing God and of serving God in a special way.

The Bible says, "*In a great house there are not only vessels of gold and silver but also of wood and earthenware, and some for noble use, and some for ignoble. If any one purifies himself from what is ignoble, then he will be a vessel for noble use, consecrated and useful to the master of the house, ready for any good work. So shun youthful passions and aim at righteousness, faith, love, and peace, along with those who call upon the Lord from a pure heart*" (2 Timothy 2:20-22).

God's house is a great house. There are various vessels in it. All the vessels are not made of the same material. Some are of gold and silver, and others of wood and earthenware. The material of which the vessel is made does not really matter, since the vessel does not make itself. It is made by the Lord. Two possible uses are open to each vessel.

The use of the vessel will depend not on what material it is made of, but on whether the vessel has purified itself from what is ignoble in it. So we have:

1. Gold vessels that have an ignoble (impure) element in them.
2. Silver vessels that also have an ignoble element in them.
3. Wooden vessels that have an ignoble element in them.
4. Earthen vessels that have an ignoble element in them.

God will use any vessel that purifies itself from that which is ignoble and consecrates itself to the Master's use (and is available and ready to be used). We can put it out this way: we shall consider three vessels in each class:

Vessel	**Test of self purification**	**Consequence (Result)**	**Test of consecration (availability to God)**	**Consequence (Result)**
Gold Vessel 1	Purifies itself	Qualifies	Consecrates itself	Used by the Master
Gold Vessel 2	Purifies itself	Qualifies	Does not consecrate itself	Not used by the Master
Gold Vessel 3	Does not purify itself	Disqualified		
Silver Vessel 1	Does not purify itself	Disqualified		
Silver Vessel 2	Purifies itself	Qualifies	Does not consecrate itself	Not used by the Master
Silver Vessel 3	Purifies itself	Qualifies	Consecrates itself	Used by the Master
Wooden Vessel 1	Purifies itself	Qualifies	Consecrates itself	Used by the Master
Wooden Vessel 2	Purifies itself	Qualifies	Does not consecrate itself	Not used by the Master
Wooden Vessel 3	Does not purify itself	Disqualified		
Earthen Vessel 1	Does not purify itself	Disqualified		
Earthen Vessel 2	Purifies itself	Qualifies	Does not consecrate itself	Not used by the Master
Earthen Vessel 3	Purifies itself	Qualifies	Consecrates itself	Used by the Master

Usefulness to God does not depend on the type of vessel. All vessels can be used. All impure vessels that refuse to purify themselves are automatically disqualified from use by the Master of the house. They may be used by the servant, etc, but not by the Master. He, being pure, will not use a dirty vessel. Dirt from which purification is needed has to do with the sins of the flesh and character defects.

It is possible for very many golden vessels (very gifted people) to be eliminated because of their sin, while God uses earthen vessels (less gifted people) who are pure. God will not say, "Well, let me just use the vessel because it is gifted. I will ignore its deliberate sin and its deliberate refusal to repent and part with sin." He will not close His eyes to grave character faults about which the believer is prepared to do nothing because the individual concerned has many natural talents and many spiritual gifts. He will prefer to wait, to suspend His action, until He finds those who are pure.

God wants purity from the heart. He is not interested in empty confessions of purity.

He looks not at the lips but at the heart. He looks not at outward actions, but at the actions of the heart.

God disqualifies no one. All start the new life with some elements of ignobility. Each one chooses whether or not to be pure. God has no favourites. If anyone is not used, it will never be because he was not gifted. It will be because he compromised with sin.

Someone can compromise with sin and still appear as if he were being used by God. That is the judgement of men and not of God; for man looks at outward action and work but God looks at inward action and work.

From the moment that a person decided that he will not make progress in the School of Holiness, he has also decided that God should not use him again. God honours his decision and the transaction is sealed. Is that the position in which you are? God can use you again if you will pay the price.

AVAILABILITY

It is sad to know that not all who purify themselves are used. Some purify themselves, but do not make themselves ready. They are not available. They do not present themselves to God as available to be used. There is no sin in their lives and they have made progress in the School of Character Formation, but they either are preoccupied with trifles and, therefore, "majoring in minors", or they lack spiritual ambition.

The pure vessels that are used are those that purify themselves and, in addition, consecrate themselves to be used by the Master of the house. This consecration means that the clean vessel presents itself to God and begs to be allowed to serve Him, even if only in a small way. We shall develop this theme of availability later on in another chapter.

FURTHER REVELATION AND THE DISTINCTIVE MINISTRY

When Moses complied with God's requirements for holiness, God revealed Himself to him further. He said to him, "*I am the God of your father, the God of Abraham, the God of Isaac and the God of Jacob*" (Exodus 3:6). God had gone further in Self-revelation. He had introduced Himself to Moses. Moses now knew the God who had spoken to him a bit more. It was not yet complete revelation, but progress had been made.

DISTINCTIVE MINISTRY

God then told Moses what the problem was. He stated it clearly:

1. He had come down to deliver the people out of the hand of the Egyptians.
2. He had come to bring them to a land flowing with milk and honey.

That was the distinctive ministry to which He was calling Moses.

It was clearly stated and presented in such a way that Moses under-stood it. God never speaks to people in a way that leaves doubts in their minds. He is always specific and clear. If anyone missed God's way, it would never be because God made it foggy.God wanted Moses to understand the situation as He understood it and to have the same feelings for the suffering sons of Jacob that He had. I believe Moses entered into very deep feelings of pain with the suffering children of Israel. He identified himself so completely with them that he finally "gave himself away" for them and accepted to be disqualified that they might be spared and allowed to enter into the Promised Land.

The sad thing about what is carried on in the name of ministry today is that it is carried out by people who have kept a safe distance from those to whom they are ministering. This results in barrenness. When an evangelist feels the agony of a lost soul on judgement day, his message will be different. If a man talks to sinners about sin without any identification in his heart with the agony of the bondage in which the depraved person is, he will not be of much help to him. Jesus, the Lord of all glory, became the Friend of sinners in order that He might bring them to God. He was fully identified with the sinner without taking part in the fleeting pleasures of their sin. The problem is that some people confuse indulgence in sin with identification with the sinner in his need. The Lord never did that. When people refused to repent, He wept. When they died, He wept and when they rejoiced, He rejoiced with them.

How do you react when after an evangelistic message, sinners refuse to respond to the Saviour? Do you feel ashamed because of the loss of face or is your heart broken because of their impending doom? Where are preachers whose hearts are broken over the lost? Where are those who would pray and pray because their hearts are broken over the lost? Oh that God would move in the power of the Holy Spirit and replace technical praying with prayers that come out of broken hearts! Such praying will produce results where dry-eyed praying has failed. However, the tears must come from the heart and not just from the eyes. They must be accompanied by a life that is set on doing all for the sake of the lost.

Distinctive Ministry and Titles

The Lord chose Moses and gave him a distinctive ministry. Moses did not become God's servant by personal choice. It was not a general invitation that God had thrown out to which Moses responded and was found to be the best of the candidates that applied. Moses was given that ministry. In some sense, he had no choice. No believer is ever a servant of the Lord by personal choice. His service is not a kind of voluntary service. The cross put an end to the rights of anyone to selfish pleasure, and condemns all the saved to become servants of God.

However, God did not give Moses a title. He remained Moses and He always addressed him as Moses. With regard to others, some-times He addressed him as "My servant Moses."

God gives ministry and the greatest title that He gives is "Servant." Today people are scrambling for titles. They call themselves by all kinds of names. They say, I am Pope X," "Archbishop Y," "Bishop Z," "Evangelist N," "Pastor M," "Prophet B," etc. They scramble for these titles and fight for them and know no peace in their hearts. These titles are not from God. They are from men. Those who receive distinctive ministries do without worldly titles. A man with a pastoral ministry should carry out that ministry and never bother to add the title "pastor" to his name. All the other ministers should do the same. They should each remain Brother K or P or Q. That is how they will be called on the Day of Reckoning. On that Day many who bear the title evangelist will find that they themselves needed to have been evangelized.

Distinctive Ministry and Public Show

The thing about religious titles is that people need them and use them for show. A distinctive ministry needs not to be public. God does not need to tell people, "I have given this person this specific ministry." Distinctive ministry can be a private ministry. Anna the prophetess was given the distinctive ministry of fasting and praying until the Hope of Israel was revealed. Simeon had the distinctive ministry of waiting on God until the Lord Jesus was brought to the temple; and when He was brought there, his distinctive ministry to the Lord and to the Lord's people was accomplished, and he said, "Lord, lettest thou thy servant depart in peace," because the ministry was fulfilled. He had done what God had called him to do almost unnoticed by anyone except God.

A certain believer in the United States of America received a distinctive ministry from the Lord to pray every Friday night until Saturday morning all alone in a chapel for five years according to very specific instructions. She knew clearly that the Lord had called her to that ministry. From that day when she heard God's voice and received that ministry, it became the one thing in her life. She spent the rest of the week preparing spiritually for that Friday night vigil with God. She judged everything by its impact on her fellowship with God and that weekly night of prayer. She went on in the loneliness of her ministry unknown to the advertising world of religious politi-cians and showmen. After five years, on a Friday night, she went to the chapel to pray as usual, but she could not pray. She was surprised, but then she remembered that the five years were over and so she thanked the Lord for enabling her to be faithful and then went back home. The next week the Holy Spirit came down in great might in that formerly cold and formal assembly, and many were filled with the Holy Spirit, and revival broke out and spread to many assemblies. That Sunday when the revival broke out one man was preaching. His name was carried on papers as a great revivalist! However, God knew who the revivalist was and on the day of reckoning she will be greatly rewarded, whereas that preacher may go unrewarded unless he, too, was a man who paid the price in his own walk with God.

God may call someone or some people to the distinctive ministry of praying for some servant of God or for some ministry. I will never forget the impact of the life of Brother Nash on me. He was called by the Lord, not to preach, but to be the force behind the ministry of the famous revivalist Finney. He followed Finney wherever he went and, while Finney preached, he prayed. God did very great things through the ministry of Finney. Was it because he was very great? We acknowledge that he was consecrated. However, part of the answer to Finney's unusual success was this private prayer giant who received from the Lord the distinctive ministry of following Finney all over and paying the price in prayer. Finney will be rewarded on that day, but I believe that Brother Nash will also receive a great reward, for, whereas Finney was seen by God and man, Nash was seen mainly by principalities and powers. Finney received all the praise and sometimes the insults from men. Nash received no praise from men. Finney was well known by men. Nash was known only to God. Both laboured one in public and the other in private but both laboured. Finney's task was a little easier than Nash's; for Finney sometimes had men as his enemies, whereas Nash constantly had principalities and powers as his enemies. Together as a team, they did a great work for God. They both finished their ministries with joy. We thank God for each one of them. My prayer is that the Lord should again call many to the private but distinctive ministries, especially those of prayer and waiting on God. These to me are the most needed ministries in the church today. The twenty-four elders never leave God's presence. They wait on Him. Theirs is a most far-reaching ministry. Shall we find their equivalent in the Church on earth today? Will carnal activity give way to spiritual waiting on God? Lord, help us.

About the private ministries where the minister is not seen and not fêted, I want to say that the glory about them is the fact that their very nature eliminates self-seeking men. They do not provide room for those who desire to glorify the flesh or who want to see immediate results. They are carried out by men who have died to the opinions and applauses of man, by men who are prepared to stand the scrutiny that goes with living in God's immediate presence and leaving all reward to Him who sees in secret.

Oh that God would raise such men in Yaounde, in Cameroon, in Nigeria, in all of Africa, and in the whole world! (Father, do it. Do it quickly, Father, for if Thou dost not do it, all Thy teachers, pastors, prophets, evangelists, and apostles, now in desperate need of prayer backing will fail Thee. Oh Father, out of Thy love for the

Lord Jesus and for His Bride-elect, do it.)

Distinctive Ministry and Personal Inadequacy

Normally, when a person receives a distinctive ministry from the Lord, there will be a deep sense of entire unworthiness for the task. (I am amazed by the fact that people scramble for spiritual office. Such people are totally blind and very unfit for ministry. They have just not understood what it is all about). When the Lord called Moses and gave him the ministry that He had for him, the first words that came from him were, "*Who am I that I should go to Pharaoh, and bring the sons of Israel out of Egypt?*" (Exodus 3:11). He had learned his lesson in the School of Humiliation well! He was saying, "I am unworthy. I am unfit for this task. It is beyond me. "Those who clearly receive ministries from the Lord by revelation see their inadequacy. They may be very gifted and very talented, but they will realize that this is spiritual ministry that can only be done in the power of the Holy Spirit, and that flesh, human methods, human training, and human techniques will fail utterly. Fools rush to ask for what they cannot do.

When a man sees the glory of God, the magnitude of the call and the high demands of an uncompromising God and sees himself in all his weakness and failure, he will say like Isaiah, "Woe is me." However, when a person has that kind of feeling it shows that he is the right man for the ministry. Why is that so? It is so because all that can be done with natural strength, natural ability, and other merely human attributes, is not a work of God.

When a man sees his inadequacy, he has discovered that spiritual ministry can only be carried out by the intervention of God who, out of mercy, would pour out His Holy Spirit without measure. Such a person will then depend absolutely on the Lord and will do everything to pay the full price for the Lord to work. Those who count on themselves only, or who count partly on the Lord and partly on themselves, or on something else, will not wait on the Lord to the same extent and will, consequently, see less of God's work done.

There are some that are spiritually impotent today who think that another year in the Bible school will remedy their impotence. Others think that another degree will do it. Some even think that a more modern meeting place with a large organ and a big choir will do it. This is unquestionable folly. Spiritual power belongs to God and, because God is everywhere, those who pay the price will receive power. Without the price paid, ten Bible schools, ten degrees, the most modern meeting place, the most modern organ, and a choir of ten thousand will only fill him with pride, but not power.

God's Answer to Spiritual Inadequacy

When Moses said, "Who am I that I should go to Pharaoh and bring the sons of Israel out of Egypt?" God answered back with a word of assurance. He said to Moses, "I will be with you." It was God's original purpose to give that to Moses as the only guarantee His presence with him. God was saying to Moses, "I have come down to deliver them. I will do it through you. I will be in you to do it. I will be the One acting. If I could fail, you would fail, but because I cannot fail, you will not fail."

God was saying to him, "You go. My presence is enough for you. May God open the eyes of all to whom He has committed distinctive ministries to see that His presence is enough and that all that they need is found in Him. Many today feel that they have the Lord Jesus but that He is not enough. They, therefore, look outside the Lord Jesus for something that will give them sufficiency. This is sad!

God calls people to impossible tasks. He calls people to that which they will never do on their own. He does this so that when the task is accomplished, it will be obvious that He did it all.

The presence of the Lord is all that is needed for any distinctive ministry. The Lord Jesus is God's all-inclusive gift. Those who have Him need nothing else. The Hymn writer wrote:

Yea, all I need in thee to find

O Lamb of God, I come! ...

Many are not satisfied with Jesus. They want Jesus plus signs. God, in His infinite wisdom, has ordained that signs come after, that signs follow rather than go before His people. He has ordained it this way because His desire is that those to whom He has entrusted distinctive ministries should walk by faith and not by sight.

Those who walk by faith will have signs following. Those who want to walk by signs will not go far. God asked Moses to go ahead and signs would follow.

Even at the present there is an inward sign the assurance of the Holy Spirit that all that God has promised will come to pass. There is that inward peace that He imparts to His servants to assure them that they are in the right place and that He will never leave them. This is something in the human spirit of the servant of God that causes him to be unmoved in the face of great difficulties while all around are losing their heads. God, furthermore, told Moses, "*Go and tell the people, 'I AM has sent me to you'*" (Exodus 3:14). The God who is I AM is available for the needs of all His servants.

- If their need is power, He says, "I am your Power," and becomes their power.

- If they are lonely, He says, "I am your Friend."

- If they are weary, He says, "I am your Comforter."

- If there are great obstacles, He says, "I am the One who takes away all obstacles." He is everything that His servants need.

The question is, "Will His servants take Him for that and move ahead, or will they wait behind and look for this and that sign?" We know that Moses asked for signs, and that Gideon placed his fleece before God, and that the apostles cast lots to find Judas's replacement. There is nothing very wrong in these things. However, they betray spiritual babyhood. For God's promises are more than all the miracles that are possible; for, when miracles cease, He is there. So the spiritually mature choose to walk by faith and not by sight, and they satisfy God's heart as others can never do.

God, make me into such a person! Lord, make us into such people.

Distinctive Ministry and God's Methods

God said to Moses, "*Go and gather the elders of Israel together and say to them, the Lord, the God of your fathers, the God of Abraham, of Isaac, and of Jacob, has appeared to me, saying, 'I have observed you and what has been done to you in Egypt; and I promise that I will bring you up out of the affliction of Egypt, to the land of the Canaanites, the Hittites, the Amorites, the Perizzites, the Hivites, and the Jebusites, a land flowing with milk and honey.' And they will hearken to your voice; and you and the elders of Israel shall go to the king of Egypt and say to him, 'The Lord, the God of the Hebrews, has met with us; and now, we pray you, let us go a three days' journey into the wilderness, that we may sacrifice to the Lord our God.' I know that the king of Egypt will not let you go unless compelled by a mighty hand. So I will stretch out my hand and smite Egypt with all the wonders which I will do in it; after that he will let you go. And I will give this people favour in the sight of the Egyptians; and when you go, you shall not go empty, but each woman shall ask of her neighbour, and of her who sojourns in her house, jewellery of silver and of gold, and clothing, and you shall put them on your sons and on your daughters; thus you shall despoil the Egyptians*" (Exodus 3:16-22).

Here, God spelled out how Moses was to go about with the first step in the ministry which He had given to him. He did not give him the ministry, withdraw, and tell him to use whatever methods he thought were convenient. No. He gave him the ministry and He spelled out what was to be done. In this way Moses was not allowed to bring his own opinions into it. God's work done God's way always works.

My counsel to all who receive distinctive ministries from the Lord is, "Wait before Him to receive His method for accomplishing that ministry. Do not rush away just upon receiving something to do. If God does not tell you how it is to be done, ask Him." Sometimes He says, "You, go. I will show you how you are to do it later on." That will be an indication that it is not yet time for you to begin. When that time comes, you will receive further instructions from Him. Do not receive a work from the Lord and then say, "Well, this work resembles that which that person did some years ago. I will go and find out how he did it and then I will do it like he did, perhaps it will work." To think and to act that way is folly.

Distinctive Ministry and Co-Workers

The Lord said to Moses, "*Is there not Aaron, your brother, the Levite? I know that he can speak well, and behold, he is coming out to meet you, and when he sees you he will be glad in his heart. And you shall speak to him and put the words in his mouth; and I will be with your mouth and with his mouth, and will teach you what you shall do. He shall speak for you to the people; and he shall be a* mouth for you, and you shall be to him as God" (Exodus 4:14-16).

There are some distinctive ministries that God gives which the person can accomplish alone. There are others which cannot be accomplished without co-workers. This passage tells us something about co-workers.

- The one to whom the ministry is given should ask for co-workers.
- God will make co-workers available.
- God will choose each co-worker.
- The one who receives the ministry is to speak to each co-worker, inviting him to the work.
- The one who receives the ministry is to put his words (those words which he received from the Lord about the ministry and how it is to be carried out) into the mouth of each co-worker, so that each co-worker will see very clearly what the ministry is and how it is to be carried out.
- God is committed to being with the co-worker as He will be with the one who has received the ministry.
- The co-worker works for God, but is responsible to the one to whom the ministry is first revealed. God said, "He shall speak for you to the people, and he shall be a mouth for you, and you shall be to him as God." Some may think that it is not right that they should speak for some other human being and be a mouth for him and that another human being should be to them as God. They say, "I

want to be independent. I want to speak directly for God. I shall be God's mouthpiece directly. I will deal directly with God." This may sound like spirituality, but it is carnality. It is pride. It is sin. God has a hierarchy in all that He does. He places some above others in function, in ministry. It is not a matter of who is better than the other. It is just that to establish order in ministry, He chooses to place some before the others.

All angels are not of the same rank, yet all are holy and all serve God. All ministries are not the same. God has placed the apostolic ministry first, then the ministry of prophets, etc. In fact, "*He has appointed in the church first apostles, second prophets...*" (1 Corinthians 12:28). This is order. To refuse the place which God has given you in a ministry in order to seek another one that you consider more important is rebellion.

The helper deals directly with the one he helps in the ministry. He receives instructions from that person about the ministry and should obey them, considering them as coming from the Lord. However, in his personal relationship with God, he deals directly with the Lord.

- The co-worker is as important to God and to the ministry as the person who receives the ministry from the Lord. They may do different things in the ministry, but each has an invaluable contribution to make, and each will receive his reward according to his faithfulness.

- The co-worker must be loyal to the one whom he is helping. Disloyalty to him will be regarded as disloyalty to God. Miriam questioned, "*Has the Lord indeed spoken only through Moses? Has he not spoken through us also?*" (Numbers 12:2). God dealt with her immediately for her attitude.

- The co-worker must forget his own opinions, ideas, and inclinations. He must carry out the opinions, ideas, and inclinations that are given to him by the person with whom he is co-working. Since this person has forsaken his own opinions, ideas, and inclinations, they will all be doing what God wants done.

- If a co-worker finds that he can no longer take instructions from the one leading the work, he should resign at once.

The Beginning of a Distinctive Ministry

All believers must continue to carry out the general ministry of the church, and they must continue to carry these out wholeheartedly until they receive their distinctive ministries from the Lord. Once the distinctive ministry is received, it must take priority over all else.

Sometimes a distinctive ministry is to be begun immediately after it is received. At other times, there is need for further waiting for more training in the Schools of God. Paul received a distinctive ministry from the Lord, but he needed three years with God in God's School in Arabia. The disciples received a distinctive ministry, but they had to wait and be clothed with power from on high.

Each one who receives a distinctive ministry must receive from the Lord when to begin it.

A distinctive ministry will always bring an end to many other ambitions. We do not know what ambitions Moses had as a shepherd. Maybe he wanted to multiply his flock a hundredfold and establish himself as a rich man. Maybe he had other ambitions. Whatever they were, one thing is clear: the encounter with God, the reception of the distinctive ministry, brought an end to all the other ambitions.

The day he received God's call, his ambition to be a great shepherd of flocks died. It received a fatal blow. The love of money, fame, etc, received a fatal wound and died. Money, fame, etc, ceased to mean anything anymore. He saw God and he saw that ministry to which he had been called. From that day on, only God mattered to him and only that ministry mattered. He put everything into knowing God and he put everything into accomplishing that ministry.

The commitment to the ministry received was total, complete. He did not ask the Lord what would happen to his flocks, just as Peter, John, and the others did not ask what would happen to their fishing business. He did not ask about a salary. He did not ask about what would become of his family. All he knew was that God, the Lord of all the universe, had condescended to call him to do a job for Him, and that call was the greatest privilege and the greatest responsibility for him.

Do you understand what I am saying? I am saying that the call to distinctive ministry brings an end to all other interests:

- professional interests,
- social interests,
- academic interests,
- spiritual interests,
- financial interests, etc.

It also brings to an end carnal caution, worldly security, and all the other guarantees of man. The person sees God; he says goodbye to all these other things, and he throws himself recklessly on

God. That is the price of a distinctive ministry, and God will not grant a distinctive ministry to people who will put it aside and pursue some cherished worldly interest. He will not give it to people who will try to accomplish it and at the same time try to gain the world. Such double-minded people are useless to God (James 1:6-8). Moses said, "Good-bye" to Midian, to his father-in-law, to his property, etc. This is absolutely essential. Have you done the same?

The Limits of Personal Ministry

Often God calls a person to do just a particular thing. He may call someone to be an evangelist to a particular tribe, town, village, nation, or continent, or He may call the person to be an evangelist to the whole world. If God calls someone to be an evangelist, he should stay within the evangelistic ministry. He should accomplish that ministry. He should not also try to be a pastor, teacher, prophet, apostle, etc. He should stay within the ministry that the Lord has called him to do for Him. There may be needs in other areas in the Body of Christ, but that is not his responsibility. He moves according to the call of God and not according to need. If he leaves the ministry to which God has called him and tries to accomplish others because of the shortage of workers, he will be doing great harm. He should pray for workers, but he should remain in the call to which the Lord has called him. He must not get involved in controversies and quarrels that concern the ministries of others. The Bible says: "*He who meddles in a quarrel not his own is like one who takes a passing dog by the ears*" (Proverbs 26:17). The dog will bite him and he will suffer a wound he could have safely avoided!

There is something more to it than just suffering unnecessarily because God has not given us time and energy for everything. Any time spent on other things is time taken away from that to which we have been called. The apostles kept themselves within the ministry of the word and prayer. They left the other things to others. People, by attempting to do everything, throw confusion into the household of God. This point is of such importance that we shall discuss it at length elsewhere.

It is not only just to stay within one's ministry, but one must also stay within the sphere of one's ministry. A person who is called by the Lord to become an evangelist to one town or village or tribe etc, but who decides on his own to become an evangelist to many towns, villages, tribes, etc, will fail God absolutely. If God calls a man to just one tribe, it means that God has a work in that tribe to occupy him up to the limits of his abilities. Should he on his own expand his ministry to people to whom God has not called him, he does much harm thus:

- He leaves his own people without the depth of care that God meant them to have as far as that ministry is concerned.

- He steps into a ministry which God had for another person at a different time and sows confusion there.

- He makes people in both places suffer loss and in this way makes the whole Kingdom of God suffer.

- He creates for the Enemy a situation to exploit for his own advantage.

This expansion beyond the limits of God is tragic beyond telling. On the other hand, a person may be called to be an evangelist to many towns, nations, and continents. Should he decide to stay in one town or nation or continent, he will fail God utterly, sow confusion into the plans of God, and leave many people outside the

Kingdom who would have entered into it had he been faithful to the extent and limit of his ministry.

So God may call a person to an evangelistic ministry in a specified area. The person should ensure that that is the ministry he has really received from the Lord and he should stay within that ministry and within the geographical spheres to which God has called him.

There is another limitation. It is the limitation of time. God may call a person to a particular ministry at a particular place for a certain length of time. It may be one day, one month, one year, or it may be ten years, or fifty. This is something that must be received from the Lord as well, without which there will be confusion; for should God call a man to spend his whole life in one place and he moves away because of the hardships practical, spiritual, etc, he would have failed God completely. On the other hand, should God call him there for one day or one year and he decides to stay there for much longer because of the blessings that the Lord was giving or because there was no one available to continue the ministry, that one would do great harm to the Lord and to His Body. Let us illustrate it from Scripture.

Philip the evangelist was involved in a great move of God in Samaria. There were conversions, healings, and deliverances and, to crown it all, the apostles came there and the Holy Spirit was poured out on these people. It was all really wonderful. There could not be a better place to stay and continue to minister. To make things even more needful for him to stay there, the converts were young and there was no one to take care of them. From a human point of view, he ought to have stayed there! However, as far as God was concerned, his ministry in Samaria was finished! An angel of the Lord said to him, "*Rise and go toward the south to the road that goes down from Jerusalem to Gaza*" (Acts 8:26). One distinctive ministry was over and another was begun. On the road to Gaza, God sent the Ethiopian to him. (This was truly a distinctive ministry, planned from the very foundations of the world, and all the details were being worked out by God.) He led him to the Lord, baptized him in water, and while the Ethiopian went away, rejoicing, you would have expected that God would lead Philip back to his beloved Samaritans. That would have been natural, human, but God did not act that way. When the Ethiopian and Philip "*came up out of the water, the Spirit of the Lord caught up Philip; and the eunuch saw him no more.... But Philip was found at Azotus, and passing on he preached the gospel to all the towns till he came to Caesarea*" (Acts 8:39-40). In Caesarea, the Lord allowed him to stay and there made a base for his further ministry as an evangelist (Acts 21:8).

Philip discharged these ministries. His was an evangelistic ministry. He moved with the Holy Spirit. When he was told, "*Rise and go . . .* " (Acts 8:26), "*He rose and went*" (Acts 8:27). By receiving clear instructions and obeying them, he stayed in the centre of God's will and fulfilled his ministry. He did not carry the burden of the churches on himself. He let the apostles do that.

Paul was having a hard time in Corinth. The Jews opposed and reviled him. He wanted to leave the town, but the Lord said to him, "*Do not be afraid, but speak and do not be silent; for I am with you, and no man shall attack you to harm you; for I have many people in this city*" (Acts 18:9-10). He obeyed and stayed there for one year and six months.

So we see that the distinctive ministry caused people to move or stay. The time varied:

- They did not move as finances dictated.
- They did not move as the political climate dictated.

- They did not move as their family situation dictated.
- Their move was not dictated by response to or rejection of the gospel. It was not dictated by the presence or absence of crowds.

They listened to the Holy Spirit and they obeyed Him, and thus they stayed within their ministries. It was the Holy Spirit, and He alone, who decided:

- the type of ministry,
- the place of ministry,
- the timing of ministry,
- the termination of ministry.

No one should allow his heart to be hooked to anything, not even to a certain ministry. No one should allow himself to be hooked to any place. No one must set his heart on any person. All hearts should be hooked on Jesus and on Him alone. The type of ministry and all that concerns it must be left to the Holy Spirit to decide. He is the Director of God's Missionary Enterprise. He selects people for the various ministries. He decides the spheres of their ministry and He sets the time limits. All who are serious obey Him.

The Completion of a Distinctive Ministry

The distinctive ministry committed by God to anyone will have a beginning in time. There will be a day when that ministry actually starts, and there will be a day when that ministry is fully accomplished.There was a day when the Lord began His public ministry. Much had happened behind the scenes in preparation, but one day He actually began the ministry. He laboured at it and one day, He said to His Father, "It is finished."

God intends that everyone to whom He has given a distinctive ministry should finish it. We have already mentioned the woman whose distinctive ministry of five years of praying all Friday night was finished and she knew it. Paul also received a distinctive ministry and he wanted it finished.

He said, "*But I do not count my life of any value nor as precious to myself, if only I may accomplish my course and the ministry which I received from the Lord Jesus, to testify to the gospel of the grace of God*" (Acts 20:24). He did accomplish his course and finish his ministry. Before he died (and not on his dying bed!) he said, "*I am already on the point of being sacrificed; the time of my departure has come. I have fought the good fight, I have finished the race, I have kept the faith*" (2 Timothy 4:6-7). Others would go on doing God's work, but that distinctive ministry that was given to Paul was com-pleted. It was finished. No one could continue it. There was nothing left that could be continued. Others could continue with what they had received from the Lord, but Paul's portion was finished.

Paul was able to finish his course and ministry. He could have died without finishing it. But praise the Lord, he did.

So, God gives distinctive ministries to people. He determines the methods to be used. He sets the limits to the ministry. Believers are to receive distinctive ministries from the Lord. They are to receive and use God's methods for the discharge of the ministry. They are to put all of themselves and all that they have into that ministry. They are to complete their ministry. Glory be to the Lord of the ministry. Amen!

CHAPTER 3

JESUS CHRIST GOD'S SUPREME SERVANT

INTRODUCTION

In the world people want to be lords. They want to boss others. They want things done for them. The Lord Jesus said, "*You know that the rulers of the Gentiles lord it over them, and their great men exercise authority over them. It shall not be so among you; but whoever would be great among you must be your servant, and whoever would be first among you must be your slave; even as the Son of man came not to be served but to serve, and give his life as a ransom for many*" (Matthew 20:25-28).

A servant is a minister. He does things for another. He gives and what he gives is received. Greatness in the Kingdom depends on giving, serving, ministering. The Lord Jesus taught that there were two levels of service: serving as a servant and serving as a slave.

1. Serving as a Servant

A servant accepts to serve. He works for a master. He receives instructions from the master and carries them out just as the master wants. He puts his opinion aside and does what the master demands. If he is content with the master, he can stay with him serving the master as long as the master wants and as long as he is satisfied. He can leave the master's service any time that he chooses to do so.

When a person wants to be great, he must serve God in this way and he must serve man in this way. This is the pathway to being great. A great man is the one who serves and not the one who receives service. The pathway to being small and unimportant is "to receive service always; to have people always do things for you," says the Lord Jesus.

2. Serving as a Slave

A slave also serves. He does everything that the servant does and in the same way. There are, however, differences between a servant and a slave.

1. A servant is paid but a slave is not paid.

2. A servant serves out of choice. He can terminate his services whenever he chooses and no one would then compel him to continue to serve. He is free. A slave has no choice. If his master is kind or unkind, good or bad, tender or hard, pleasant or unpleasant, etc, he serves him all the same. He is to serve him with all his might, irrespective of what his master is. The quality of his service is not dependent on what the master is. He must never complain. He must never disobey. The servant has working hours. He can go off and do anything he likes when he is not on duty. The slave has no working schedule. He is expected to be on duty all the time. He has no free time. He is bound to serve always.

3. A master can become dissatisfied with the servant and can dismiss him. If a slave owner is dissatisfied with him, he can kill him. The slave may only live as long as his services satisfy his master.

Jesus said, "Servants shall be great but slaves shall be first." *The first in the Kingdom of God shall be those who serve God and man as slaves. It is understandable that we are God's slaves. He has bought us and put His marks upon us. We have no choice about serving Him. It is the greatest privilege to serve Him. He is a wonderful Lord and this makes it even easier to serve Him; for He says, "My yoke is easy, and my burdens light"* (Matthew 11:30). But what about serving man? Are we prepared to serve him all the time regardless of whether he is grateful or ungrateful, pleasant or nasty? Will we serve him even when he speaks evil of us? Shall we serve him even when he persecutes us and kills us? Unless we are prepared to serve God and man in this way, we will never be first in the Kingdom! May some not say, "I will not be a first. I will just be in the Kingdom, so I will not humble myself that much." We shall look at that in detail when we treat the theme "You as a servant of God and Man." For now we say that if God has called you to be a first by serving as a slave and you run away from this to settle for something less but easy, you have forsaken your calling and failed the Lord woefully. The Lord Jesus is God's first. He served God as a slave and He served man as a slave. We shall now look at Him who is our supreme Example.

JESUS SERVED THE LORD AND MAN IN A DISTINCTIVE WAY

The Lord Jesus received from the Father a distinctive ministry. It was two-fold.

1. He was to glorify the Father.
2. He was to seek and save that which was lost.

He glorified the father

The Lord Jesus never served in order to draw attention to Himself. He served so that the Father might be glorified. He said, "*For I have come down from heaven, not to do my own will, but the will of him who sent me; and this is the will of him who sent me, that I should lose nothing of all that he has given me, but raise it up at the last day. For this is the will of my Father, that every one who sees the Son and believes in him should have eternal life; and I will raise him up at the last day*" (John 6:38-40). "*My food is to do the will of him who sent me, and to accomplish his work*" (John 4:34). "*I can do nothing on my own authority; as I hear, I judge; and my judgment is just, because I seek not my own will, but the will of him who sent me*" (John 5:30).

He sought and saved the lost

He sought and saved those who were lost in sin as His primary purpose. But he also sought and saved those who were lost in sickness and diseases. He sought and saved those who were bound by demons. He saved those who were lost in hunger by giving them food. He saved those who were lost in death by bringing them to life. He sought and saved those who were bound by hypocrisy by being an example to them, and for those who were lost in self-seeking, He saved them by a demonstration of humility.

He refused to be involved in all good things that were not part of his ministry

The Lord Jesus did very many good things, but He only did those which were an integral part of His distinctive ministry on earth. For example, He refused to become a distributor of wealth. The Bible says, "*One of the multitude said to him, 'Teacher, bid my brother divide the inheritance with me.' But he said to him, 'Man, who made me a judge or divider over you?'*" (Luke 12:13-14). He refused to be involved in political agitation. He said nothing for or against the government of the day, but submitted Himself to it. However, He confronted the religious leaders of the day and denounced their hypocrisy in very clear terms. He refused to own property. He had no place to lay His head. He refused to get married. Although He could have taught very competently on science, agriculture, art, literature, etc, He refused all these and only taught what was related to His ministry.

He obtained instructions from the father and obeyed them

Jesus was always withdrawing from the crowd to pray. In prayer He did two main things: He asked God how He was to carry out His will, and received power to carry it out. The Bible says, "*And in the morning, a great while before day, he rose and went out to a lonely place, and there he prayed*" (Mark 1:35). The multitudes were there pressing on Him, but instead of "pressing" back on them, He withdrew and first "pressed" on the Father before coming back to "press" on them. After He had fed the five thousand by a miracle, He did not stay among men in order to bathe in their praises, but He dismissed the crowd, sent the disciples before Him, and "*went up on the mountain by himself to pray*" (Matthew 14:23). He spent so much time in prayer that by evening He was still there alone and had to walk on the sea to meet them.

So Jesus was not always in public. He was often in private with God. That was the secret of His ministry. He came from the presence of God into the presence of man and back into the presence of God.

JESUS MADE ROOM FOR THE MINISTRY OF OTHERS

He did not do everything. He discerned everything. He called the twelve, trained them, and sent them out. He called the seventy, trained them and sent them out. He calls the Church and wants to train her that He may send her out. Unlike the disciples who were caught up with a party spirit, He said, "*Do not forbid him; for no one who does a mighty work in my name will be able soon after to speak evil of me. For he that is not against us is for us*" (Mark 9:39-40).

JESUS CARRIED OUT HIS MINISTRY UNDER A SENSE OF GREAT COMPULSION AND GREAT URGENCY

The ministry of the Lord Jesus was everything to Him:

1. It was the reason why He came.
2. It was His food.
3. It was His priority.
4. It was the one thing that had to be done about which there was no choice.
5. He paid the supreme price in order to accomplish it.

It was the reason why he came

The Bible says, "*And in the morning, a great while before day, he rose and went out to a lonely place, and there he prayed. And Simon and those who were with him pursued him, and they found him and said to him, 'Every one is searching for you. And he said to them, 'Let us go on to the next towns, that I may preach there also; for that is why I came out. And he went throughout all Galilee, preaching in their synagogues and casting out demons*" (Mark 1:35-39).

The Lord was having a wonderful time with His Father in prayer. It was good. It was necessary, but that was not the reason why He came. Everyone was looking for Him. Everyone wanted Him. The disciples sought Him and when they found Him, they told Him about the situation and He understood. He could not hold back. He had come to seek and to save these people. Now they were seeking Him and He felt compelled to go to them. He told them that they must all be on the move. They had to go to the other towns so that He should preach there also; for that was why He came. He refused to allow preparation to take up the place of action. He did not only talk, He acted. He went with the disciples throughout all of Galilee, ministering. He did not just go through part of Galilee. He went throughout all of Galilee, fulfilling His ministry. His ministry was the reason why He came and He gave that the priority.

It was his food and his priority

Even before the Lord Jesus began His public ministry, He settled very clearly what place food was going to occupy in His life. After He was baptized at the Jordan (both into water and into the Holy Spirit) He fasted for forty days. He was saying to the desire for food, "You will not rule. I am the Ruler." He thus put food and all the needs of His physical body into the second place and remained the Controller of His being. Later on when there was real desire for food, the Enemy wanted to use that to cause Him to sin, but He remained Victor as He proclaimed, "*Man shall not live by bread alone but by every word that proceeds from the mouth of God*" (Matthew 4:4). He again put bread, food, and the needs of the physical body into the place of servant and not that of master. He said: "Food is good. It is necessary, but there is one thing that is indispensable every word that proceeds from the mouth of God."

This was not an attitude which He adopted for just some time. He maintained it all His life. Once, He left Judea and departed again for Galilee and had to pass through Samaria. He thus came to a city of Samaria called Sychar. He had walked for a long time and was weary with the journey. His disciples went away into the city to buy food. He could have sat there with all His thoughts buried in His tiredness and the expectation of food so as to be oblivious of all the needs around. However, He did not do that. A woman of Samaria soon came around, and when He saw her need, He began to minister to her. So deep was His involvement with her that the weariness of the body and the need for food were lost in the one ministry of reaching out to that lost woman. The Bible says, "*Meanwhile the disciples besought him, saying, 'Rabbi, eat.' But he said to them, 'I have food to eat of which you do not know.' So the disciples said to one another, 'Has any one brought him food?' Jesus said to them, 'MY FOOD IS TO DO THE WILL OF HIM WHO SENT ME, AND TO ACCOMPLISH HIS WORK'*" (John 4:31-34).

The Lord was living and serving at a plane which the disciples did not understand. He fed on the Word. He fed on the Father and this ministered to Him at a level that the disciples could not yet understand. They thought that if He no longer needed food, someone must have given Him food. Yes, Someone gave Him food, His heavenly Father fed Him. However, it was not food for His body. It was food for His spirit and He was satisfied. Some people eat in order to do the business of life. This is normal. Others make eating the business of life. This is abnormal. For the Lord, the one business of life, which was doing the will of His Father, was food itself. This is supernatural.

The Lord Jesus thus lived in this supernatural dimension in which doing the Father's will was like eating. He lived in a dimension where the whole body served the desires of His Spirit. His spirit ruled His whole body.

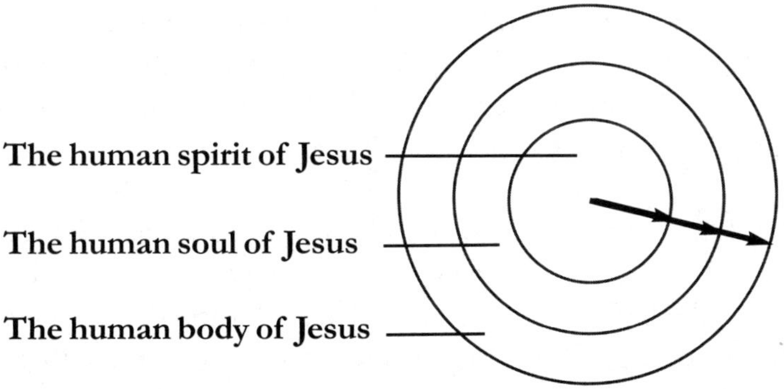

The spirit of Jesus was completely released from His soul and the desires of His body were totally subservient to the desires of His soul, so that whatever His spirit wanted, was carried out. So when the Father fed Him afresh with the food of His Word, He was sustained, not only in His spirit, but also in His soul and body. This is God's desire for all His other children that they, too, like the First Born, should be ruled by the desires of the spirit and not by those of the soul or body.

There is another side to the matter. The need that presented itself to Him was a need that was tied to the will of His Father and the work that He had to accomplish. This need was not food for His body, but getting the Samaritan woman into the Kingdom of God. There was, so to say, a conflict. Two needs presented themselves to Him at the same time; the needs of His body and the needs of a lost sinner. He immediately knew where the priorities had to be. He attended to the woman.

There was also a time factor involved. The needs of His body could be met later on. However, the needs of that woman could not wait. Time was running out. If her need was not met, then it might be too late. She might never have a second chance. It was then or never. Do you see how the Lord weighed things? He did not say: "This woman could be saved another day." He gave Himself, even after total exhaustion, so that she might find life there and then. May we, too, act like that. When faced with the opportunity to minister life, may we not postpone it. May we act at once because we may never have that opportunity again.

The Father had pre-ordained that that woman would be saved on that day. The Lord Jesus knew this; for He ministered in the perfection of the Father's will. So He went ahead and did the Father's will at any cost to Himself. It was not only important that she should be saved but it was also important that she should be saved then, and the price had to be paid for that. God does not only want people saved, He wants them saved at the right moment. Think of it in the following way: If God wants someone saved at twenty so that He may be sent as an apostle to some unreached tribe, what if the person who was to minister to him failed to do so for one reason or the other? What if this man then continued in sin for the next forty years and got saved at sixty? Someone may say: "Praise the Lord, he got saved all the same." Yes, we would praise the Lord that the man got saved ultimately, but what of the forty years that were lost to God's work and that were invested for the devil? What of that tribe? What of the thousands of people there who perished without Christ because that person was not saved at twenty? Is that a small matter to you? Do you see the consequence of a "small" disobedience? Do you see how far-reaching sin may be? Do you see how critical the time factor is? Do you see how necessary it is to live and act as Jesus did?

There was another reason why Jesus could not wait for another day before reaching out to this woman. It was both holy jealousy and holy anger. He was jealous that this woman was serving the devil instead of serving the Father, and He was angry that the devil dared keep someone who was created in the image of God in his ugly kingdom. Because of this jealousy and anger, the Lord could not stand her spending another day in the devil's kingdom, and so He did all He could right then to save her at once.

The Lord Jesus knew that some things could wait while others could not. He told the disciples, "*She has done a beautiful thing to me. For you always have the poor with you, and whenever you will, you can do good to them; but you will not always have me*" (Mark 14:6-7). In this way Jesus divided the things that could be done into a scale of priorities. The things of top priority that must be done, and, if there is time, the other things that may be done. To have a life without priorities may lead to specializing in the non-essentials. How is it with you? Are there priorities in your life or are you majoring in minors?

There are so many things that can be done today and many things that make demands. God wants His own to know what cannot wait. I personally think that the following can wait:

-making a name.

-making money.

But winning people into the Kingdom, being holy, total abandonment to the Lord, and doing God's will, cannot wait.

He had no choice: he did what were "musts" for him

Jesus ministered under a real sense of compulsion. Having accepted the Father's will and abandoned His, there was only one way open to Him. He expressed it by the words "I must."

1. At the tender age of twelve He told His parents, "*How is it that you sought me? Did you not know that I must be in my Father's house?*" (Luke 2:49). That was a far-reaching declaration! He expected His parents to know that being in His Father's house was a "must" for Him.

2. He retired for fellowship with His Father after a busy day. The people sought Him and came to Him, and would have kept Him from leaving them, but He said to them, "*I must preach the good news of the Kingdom of God to the other cities also; for I was sent for this purpose. And he was preaching in the synagogues of Judea*" (Luke 4 : 43-44). These people wanted to monopolise Him. They wanted to keep Him for themselves, but He said to them, "You can't do it. I have a purpose. That purpose includes other cities. I must accomplish that purpose. Do not hold Me back." Often people see a man

of God and they want to keep him. They want to own him. They want to label him as theirs and say:

He belongs to our mission.

He belongs to our denomination.

He belongs to our church, or

He belongs to our X, Y, and Z.

How carnal such actions are! Men of God belong to God. They also belong to the whole Church. They belong to the whole world. When we meet them, may we know that and may we not try to limit them. May we thank God for them and may we receive ministry from them, and then may we send them on to all of God's people and to all of God's world.

3. The Lord said, "*I have other sheep that are not of this fold; I must bring them also, and they will heed my voice. So there shall be one flock and one shepherd*" (John 10:16). There is one fold already established. There are not two folds. God knows nothing about the Pentecostal fold, the Baptist fold, the Presbyterian fold, etc. God knows the fold of His Son Jesus. Jesus, however, has other sheep that by error do not yet belong to His fold. They, perhaps, belong to someone or to something. Jesus cannot tolerate this. He must bring the other sheep so that there is one fold even as there is one Shepherd. All sheep must ask, "Where is the fold of Christ?" Then they must seek it and belong to it. Remember that God has established that there be one fold and one Shepherd. Anything that does not resemble this is terrible. Jesus will never allow two folds. There will never be another shepherd. This should make believers rethink. This whole matter of one fold and one Shepherd was so important to the Lord Jesus that He made the bringing of the other sheep that were not yet in the fold a "must." We must do the same. He, however, did not say that He would bring goats and mix them

with sheep and make one fold with them. The two are immiscible. Only folly will try to mix them up. But to separate sheep into two folds is horrible!

4. The Lord further said, "*We must work the works of him who sent me, while it is day; night comes, when no one can work*" (John 9:4).

5. "*And as Moses lifted up the serpent in the wilderness, so must the Son of man be lifted up, that whosoever believes in him may have eternal life*" (John 3:14-15).

6. The Lord of all glory said to His disciples, "*Go and tell that fox, 'Behold I cast out demons and perform cures today and tomorrow, and the third day I finish my course.' Nevertheless I must go on my way today and tomorrow and the day following; for it cannot be that a prophet should perish away from Jerusalem*" (Luke 13:32-33). Jesus was saying, "I must finish my course. Therefore, I must act today, for tomorrow there will be no time to continue."

7. "*The Son of man must suffer many things, and be rejected by the elders and chief priests and the scribes, and be killed, and on the third day be raised*" (Luke 9:22).

Yes, the Son of man:

1. Must suffer many things.
2. Must be rejected.
3. Must be killed.
4. Must be raised.

There was no option whatsoever. Let us again see the "musts" of His life. He

1. Must be in His Father's house,
2. Must preach the Good News to other cities,

3. Must bring the other sheep to His fold,

4. Must work the works of Him who sent Him while it is day,

5. Must be lifted up,

6. Must finish His course,

7. Must suffer many things, be rejected, be killed, and be raised.

The "musts" of His life were all an integral part of the supreme purpose of His mission. He came for the very things that were a Amust" for Him. He did not make any peripherial issue a central issue.

When the disciples tried to defend Him, He said, "*Put your sword into its sheath; shall I not drink the cup which the Father has given me?*" (John 18:11).

He Refused to Be Put Off by Obstacles

He chose the twelve apostles and found that one of them was a thief. He refused to be put off by thieves. He could have said, "If one of the apostles is a thief, what hope is there for the rest?"

He found that the apostles could not understand Him most of the time, yet He was not discouraged. Peter, their leader, denied Him, yet He did not lose faith in the ultimate victory of the Lord.

The unbelief of the Jews hit Him in the face wherever He went, but even that did not put Him off. What could have driven most people to despairC the hardness of heart of the religious leaders of the day and their combined efforts to put Him to death and sabotage His ministry did not faze Him.

He had faith in the power of God to accomplish His will, which was designed, not in some time of emergency, but from the foundations of the world. In refusing to be put off He was saying, "My Father is Lord. He will conquer in all these situations. He will be Lord in them all. His cause cannot be defeated. The devil will fail. His purpose will not be able to thwart the purposes of God, for the devil will soon be defeated on the cross. My Father is able to change weak and failing men into strong men of courage. He is not only able. He is willing. He will do it. I trust the Holy Spirit who resides in these disciples and who will come upon them. He is a Master in accomplishing my purpose in them. He will not fail in His job."

JESUS CARRIED OUT A DIVERSIFIED MINISTRY TO INCLUDE ALL OF THE PURPOSES THAT WERE THE OBJECT OF HIS MINISTRY

He did this by:

1. Raising the dead,
2. Healing the sick,
3. Delivering the possessed,
4. Teaching the Word,
5. Washing the disciples' feet,
6. Blessing babes,
7. Ministering to crowds,
8. Ministering to individuals,
9. Ministering in public,
10. Ministering in private,
11. Exhorting,

12. Rebuking,
13. Restoring backsliders,
14. Dying on the cross,
15. Resurrecting from the dead.

He assessed every action by its contribution to the overall purpose of His ministry.

HE MINISTERED IN UTTER HUMILITY

We have already talked about the difference between the servant and a slave. The Lord Jesus did not serve as a servant. He served as a slave. He was a slave that was doomed to die the most degrading death possible. The Bible says, "*Have this mind among yourselves, which is yours in Christ Jesus, who, though he was in the form of God, did not count equality with God a thing to be grasped, but emptied himself, taking the form of a servant, (slave) being born in the likeness of men. And being found in human form he humbled himself and became obedient unto death, even death on a cross*" (Philippians 2:5-8).

Do you see the pathway He trod? He humbled Himself. He went down. Let us sum it up this way with each arrow indicating a step downward in the path of humiliation:

The way of humiliation

He was in the form of God

↓

He became a human being by choice

↓

He chose to became a servant

↓

He chose to serve as a slave

↓

He chose to serve as a slave that must die

↓

He chose to serve as a slave that must die by the most degrading method : death uon a cross

He totally forgot His honour, reputation, etc. He was oblivious of what people thought and said. He knew that it was said, "Cursed is any one who hangs upon a tree." He, nevertheless, said, "I will be accursed. I will hang on a tree so that I may accomplish My ministry." Nothing was too low for Him, provided it was part of the reason for which He came. He sacrificed everything for the sake of His mission.

Before He went to the cross, He poured water in a basin and washed the feet of His disciples. It was the exact opposite of expected behaviour. The world advocates pride and praises the proud. The cross condemns the proud and exalts the humble. The Lord chose the way of humility. That is why the Bible says, "*Therefore, God has highly exalted him and bestowed on him the name which is above every name, that at the name of Jesus every knee should bow, in heaven and on earth and under the earth, and every tongue confess that Jesus*

Christ is Lord, to the glory of God the Father" (Philippians 2:9-11).

If you want to glorify God the Father, bow down to Jesus Christ and confess that He is Lord. Yes, the way to truly glorify God is to glorify the Son. It is as if the glory that satisfies the heart of the Father the most is not the one that is given to Him, but the one that is given to Jesus Christ. He exalted Jesus for that very purpose.

We again let each arrow up indicate a step upward into glory.

The way of exaltation

Every tongue shall confess that Christ Jesus is Lord, to the glory of God the Father

↑

At the name of Jesus every knee should bow, of thing in heaven, on eatrh and under the earth

↑

God bestowed upon Him a name which is above every name

↑

God highly exalted Him

↑

God exalted Him

↑

Goad raised Him from the dead

↑

Jesus in the depth of humiliation of death on a tree

The Lord Jesus' ministry would have been impossible, had He not humbled Himself from its beginning right to its end.

JESUS COMPLETED HIS MINISTRY

The Lord Jesus came to the world with a particular ministry in mind. He devoted Himself to it and refused to be side-tracked by secondary issues or by unrelated matters. He did what He had to do.

He said that He would labour so as to finish His course (Luke 13:32). On the cross, He finished it and proclaimed, "*It is finished.*" After that, and only after that, did He commit His spirit to the Father and die.

Glory be to His holy Name!

CHAPTER 4

SPIRITUAL AMBITION AS EXEMPLIFIED IN THE LIFE OF PAUL

WHAT IS SPIRITUAL AMBITION?

Spiritual ambition is the total desire and total commitment to be all that Christ saved one for and wants one to be. It is that desire to seek the greatest possible things for God, the desire to win the mightiest possible battles for God, the desire to put on all of Christ that is possible. It is that determination to do all for the Lord and be all that He wants one to be in the shortest possible time. Spiritual ambition includes that determination to inflict the most far-reaching damages on the kingdom of the wicked one and to do this in the shortest possible time. It is the determination to do everything that God wants done and to do it in God's way and time.

The Lord spoke to Baruch through the prophet Jeremiah, saying, "*And do you seek great things for yourself? Seek them not*" (Jeremiah 45:5). Baruch was not forbidden to seek great things. He was forbidden to seek great things for himself. Were he to seek great things for the Lord, it would have been in order. We can ask, "And do you seek great things for the Lord?" The answer will be: "Seek them."

MAN'S GREAT POTENTIALS

God created man with great potentials. He put into man enormous capacities and great abilities. These capacities can be used for the greatest good or for the greatest evil. On the other hand, they can be buried. The servant who had five talents laboured and doubled his initial capital. The one who had two did the same, but the one who had one talent buried it and there was a far-reaching loss.Every human being can, to some extent, become either faithful John or treacherous Judas, depending on what he sets his mind to do. God created us for great things and recreated us in the Lord Jesus for the greatest things.

SAUL THE ZEALOT

Even before his conversion to the Lord Jesus, Saul of Tarsus was zealous. He was born and brought up as a Jew. He became a Pharisee and put everything into his religion. He was not a man of half-measures. He knew nothing of half-hearted commitment. His religion possessed him. He was taken up with it and he gave all that he was and all that he had to it. He was anxious that the purity of his religion should remain untarnished. He wanted all to belong to it. He was intolerant of any other religion. Endowed with many natural talents and a good education, he invested these into his religion. He himself put it this way: "*I persecuted the church of God violently and tried to destroy it; and I advanced in Judaism beyond many of my own age among my people, so extremely zealous was I for the traditions of my fathers*" (Galatians 1:13-14).

As a Jew, Saul had spiritual ambition. That ambition was clearC to uphold the course of Judaism. He gave his all to that ambition by:

1 . Opposing everything that was not in accordance with his faith actively, violently. Do you see this? He went on his own initiative to ask papers of the religious leaders so as to go and carry out the raid against believers in Damascus.

2. Doing all he could to destroy the Church.

3. Making more progress than others in Judaism.

4. Being extremely zealous after his religion.

5. Being extremely mad in opposing the Church.

His commitment was described by such words as:

extremely mad,

violently,

advanced beyond many,

extremely zealous.

No one can be said to truly possess spiritual ambition whose life and commitment cannot be described by such words and phrases. The sad thing is that easy-going unbelievers often turn out to be easy-going believers. Saul was a zealot and when he became Paul, he was red-hot for the Lord.

SPIRITUAL AMBITION ROOTED IN REVELATION AND COMMISSION

Before his conversion, Paul had natural zeal. After his conversion, he had spiritual zeal. The difference between the two is that one came out of his religious nature and was, therefore, mistaken. The other had its origin in God. It was zeal for God's revealed purpose. The Lord had said to him, "*I have appeared to you for this purpose, to appoint you to serve and bear witness to the things in which you have seen me and to those in which I will appear to you, delivering you from the people and from the Gentiles to whom I send you to open their eyes, that they may turn from darkness to light and from the power of Satan to God, that they may receive forgiveness of sins and a place among those who are sanctified by faith in me*" (Acts 26:16-18).

The Lord revealed Himself to Paul and He gave him a very clear charge. He said to him, "You are My appointee for witness and service. You shall carry out the following charge:

You shall bear witness to the things you have seen and will see of Me. You are to open the people's eyes with one purpose in view: that they may turn from darkness to light, from the power of Satan to God, that they may receive forgiveness of sins and an inheritance among the sanctified.

Paul received this from the Lord. He then made that which he had received the one reason for living. He made the accomplishment of that God-given task the one reason for living. The Lord of heaven had chosen him and given him a work to do. That was all. He made that the one reason for living for him.

TERMINATION WITH ALL ELSE

Paul obviously had other ambitions before that day when the Lord called him. He perhaps wanted to make a name as a great Pharisee. This was an ambition that was ultimately against the gospel. So he let it die there and then. He abandoned it completely. He might have had other ambitions: to be a great scholar and carry out enormous research to help humanity make academic and social progress. That ambition was not against Christ. He might have then wanted to serve the Jews and bring them into the Kingdom of God. In fact, he had a burden that way; for he himself said, "*I have great sorrow and unceasing anguish in my heart ... for the sake of my brethren, my kinsmen by race*" (Romans 9:2-3). He again said, "*Brethren, my heart's desire and prayer to God for them is that they may be saved*" (Romans 10:1). He had this passion for his people and could preferentially have loved to go to them. God's will for him, however, was the Gentiles. He, therefore, forsook his natural inclinations and obeyed the Lord.

He himself said, "*But whatever gain I had, I counted as loss for the sake of Christ*" (Philippians 3:7). However, it did not end there. He went on, for he said, "*Indeed, I count everything as loss because of the surpassing worth of knowing Christ Jesus my Lord. For his sake I have suffered the loss of all things, and count them as refuse in order that I may gain Christ*" (Philippians 3:7-8).

Paul counted everything as loss. He counted everything as refuse, as dung. Something happened in Paul that brought him to a position in which if a person had made him a billionaire, a Head of State, a Nobel prize winner, or any other honour known in the world of men, he would have counted it as rubbish. He would have counted it as dung. From the day that God gave him a charge, all the world's offers became absolutely senseless. However, the call of God on him was only part of the issue. There was something greater and higher. He could count all things as dung, as secondary, because God had called him to something else and that to which God had called him had become primary. He called everything else dung primarily because of the surpassing knowledge of the Lord Jesus. Knowing Jesus was worth more than all the world put together. Jesus was everything to him. Jesus was enough. He, like the hymn writer, said:

"Yea, all I need in Thee to find,

0 Lamb of God, I come, I come."

To have Jesus was to have everything and to know Jesus was to know everything. Then to serve Jesus was the one reason for living.Had Paul not had Jesus and desired Jesus, all the other things would have made sense, a lot of sense. For those who do not know Jesus or who know Him too dimly, being a billionaire, a Head of State, a Nobel Prize winner, etc, makes a lot of sense and these things are pursued by them to varying degrees. All attempts at leaving them will prove false and all declarations about how they are not sought will prove to be nothing but words; for the heart will still be bound and hooked to them. They will run away physically from them, but their hearts will yet be bound to them. When to them, however, Jesus becomes all in all, and the surpassing knowledge of knowing Him becomes life's goal, there will be no place whatsoever for these things. There will be no competition.

Paul thus terminated with these things. He terminated with the world. He said, "*But far be it from me to glory except in the cross of our Lord Jesus Christ, by which the world has been crucified to me, and I to the world*" (Galatians 6:14).

Do you see what happened? The world and all the attractive things in it were dead to Paul. They could offer him nothing. He, too, was dead to them. He could offer them nothing. The world did not count on him. He was dead. He did not count on the world. It was crucified and, in a sense, dead to him.

There was, therefore, this radical termination, not only with the world, but also with the "*self' Paul. That self-seeking "self' was also smashed. He could gladly testify, "I have been crucified with Christ; it is no longer I who live, but Christ who lives in me; and the life I now live in the flesh I live by faith in the Son of God, who loved me and gave himself for me*" (Galatians 2:20). He was crucified. It was not him living but Christ living in him. He lived then by faith in the Son of God. To him, this was not just a doctrine to be understood: It was an experience, a daily experience. The self-life was radically dealt with; so that it might no longer interfere with his supreme ambition.

He had passions of all kinds resulting from his flesh, but what did he do about these? He crucified them. He put them to death. He could, out of his own experience, say, "*Those who belong to Christ Jesus have crucified the flesh with its passions and desires*" (Galatians 5:24).

He crucified some legitimate passions like the passions for a wife, for a home, and for children. He crucified the passion to be loved, comforted, understood, etc. He crucified all of them and went on to love the one Object of his love and to serve the One he loved so well.

Without this radical termination with everything else, Paul would have failed in his ambition. He would not have accomplished it because he would have been divided at heart. He would have been confused when faced with a situation where to speak the truth would have stood in the way of a coveted promotion. He would have failed when the Lord wanted one thing and the world, the flesh, etc, wanted another. He, as it were, separated himself radically and totally from all that could hinder success. When faced with a choice, he weighed its impact on his life's goal. He did not just do all that he could legitimately do. He did only that which helped him to accomplish his goal. He said, "*All things are lawful for me, but not all things are helpful. All things are lawful for me, but I will not be enslaved by anything*" (1 Corinthians 6:12). Again he said: "*All things are lawful, but not all things build up*" (1 Corinthians 10:23). He ever sought, not the lawful or the permitted, but that which would help him and build him up; so that he might best accomplish his goal.

Hence Paul put aside all that could stand in his way. He terminated with all else. All whose ambitions are like his cannot but terminate with everything else; for divided hearts are useless to God. May we repeat that divided hearts are useless to God.

Is your heart divided? If it is, you are useless to God and you are useless for God. The greatest insult that can be poured out on Divine Omnipotence is to serve Him with a divided heart.

If your heart is divided, everything about you will be confused. The sum total of your life will be great failure, complete failure.

THE INESCAPABLE DISCIPLINE

Paul had received a commission from the Lord. There was something to do for the Lord as his secondary objective. There was the Lord to know as his primary objective. The two were intertwined. He could not know the Lord and not serve Him, and he could not serve the Lord profoundly without knowing Him intimately. We have seen that Paul had to say a final goodbye to the world and all that it offered. He also said goodbye to all the passions in his life, so that he could have only one passion knowing Jesus and serving Him.

He had one more thing to do. He had to get his body not to stand in his way but to serve him. He said, "*Every athlete exercises self-control in all things. They do it to receive a perishable wreath, but we an imperishable. Well, I do not run aimlessly, I do not box as one beating the air; but I pommel my body and subdue it, lest after preaching to others I myself should be disqualified*" (1 Corinthians 9:25-27).

Paul exercised discipline over his thoughts, his emotions, his words, his body, his all. He got his body to obey him. He got sleep, hunger, etc, all under control. He was a disciplined man.

As part of the discipline, he did not involve himself in everything that presented itself to him. He did not do good things. He refused better things. He concentrated on the best things that contributed the most towards the goal to which he had dedicated his life.

He did not run aimlessly. The call of God on him was ever before him. Knowing Christ and serving Him was all that mattered to him. He knew his enemies the devil, the world and the flesh. These stood in the way of his winning Christ and he kept his blows at these enemies. He did not attack the social, medical, educational, racial, or other societal problems. He kept all his blows at the three-fold enemy. He refused all secondary goals. He turned his back to many material goods. He kept his eyes on the Lord Jesus and the work to which He had called him, and with a disciplined body, disciplined in everything and in all things, he set on on his life's goal.

He assessed everybody and everything by their impact on his goal. He kept a vigilant watch. He would often ask: "Will doing this thing get me nearer my goal?" He would at the close of a day ask himself, "Am I nearer my goal?".

PAUL'S SPIRITUAL AMBITION WAS GOAL-DIRECTED

In talking about Paul's spiritual ambition, it should not be understood that he had any other ambition. His one ambition was Christ. He did not have a professional ambition and a spiritual ambition. Had that been the case, he would have been divided at heart and failed God utterly; for no one can serve two masters.

His one ambition was clear. He could assess the progress he was making in the direction of accomplishing his ambition. His one ambition, his only ambition, was to know Christ and to serve Him.

A. Knowing Christ included:

1. Knowing Him as Lord.
2. Knowing the power that brought Him back to life from the dead (the power of the resurrection).
3. Knowing fellowship with Him in His suffering.
4. Knowing conformity to Him in His death.
5. Knowing conformity to Him in His resurrection.

He wanted, therefore, to be as perfect in character and personality as Christ was. In knowing Christ in this way, he was compelled, out of a holy jealousy for the Lord whom he loved, to do two things:

1. Hate the Enemy with all his might, which included hating:

   a. the devil,

   b. the world, and

   c. the flesh.

2. Be possessed by a holy anger against all activities of the Enemy. Therefore, wherever he saw a work of the devil that stood in the way of the purpose for which Christ called him, he destroyed it mercilessly.

B. Serving Christ included:

1. Preaching Christ to all people, everywhere within the limits of his distinctive ministry, with special emphasis on those places and those peoples among whom He had not yet been named.

2. Building the Church of Christ so that it is perfect:

   a. without spot,

   b. without blemish,

   c. without wrinkle.

This meant that he was determined to bear fruit, not thirty or sixty-fold, but a hundredfold. He was determined not only to get the best quality for His Lord, but also the largest quantity. He was, therefore, quality and quantity conscious.

NORMAL PATTERN OF SPIRITUAL AMBITION

We say very definitely that spiritual ambition will include that desire to:

1. Know Christ.
2. Know all the power of the resurrection.
3. Know fellowship with Christ in His suffering.
4. Know fellowship with Him in His death.
5. Know conformity to Him in His resurrection.
6. Know total conformity in character to Christ.
7. Know a holy jealousy for the glory of God.
8. Know a holy anger against the devil and all his works.

This is basic and no one can exempt himself from this aspect of spiritual ambition. In each case it will be to know as Christ knew; for He has called us to His fullness. He himself said, "*You, therefore, must be perfect, as your heavenly Father is perfect*" (Matthew 5:48). Could He have commanded us to a perfection that is impossible? He used the word, " must." Could He have been placing a "must" before us that was not possible? Can the failure of the Church collectively and the saints individually over the years change the requirements of Christ and His God? Does the Lord not still expect perfection?

Could the failure be rooted partly in the fact that His children do not believe that He meant what He said? If anyone begins by saying that the goal is not possible, how then will he accomplish that which he is not aiming at? I will not let any such failure lower God's standard. I acknowledge that the Lord wants perfection. I acknowl-edge that full conformity to the Father and the Son is possible. I acknowledge that failure on my part and on the part of the Church to attain to that perfection, to bear fruit a hundredfold, etc, grieves God's heart. All interpretations and watering down of Scripture that ease our consciences will not satisfy God.

Paul had this perfection, this satisfaction of the heart of God, in view. It was the sum total of His ambition. He wanted to know Christ, serve Him, and thereby attain the prize of the upward call of God in Christ Jesus. The attainment of the goal included perfection in every way and, even in his maturity, the apostle Paul said, "*Not that I have already obtained this or am already perfect; but I press on to make it my own, because Christ Jesus has made me his own. Brethren, I do not consider that I have made it my own; but one thing I do, forgetting what lies behind and straining forward to what lies ahead, I press on toward the goal for the prize of the upward call of God in Christ Jesus*" (Philippians 3:12-14).

Besides knowing Christ in His totality, spiritual ambition will also include serving Christ. This service will be the carrying out of the general ministry of the Church and the accomplishment of the distinctive ministry received from the Lord. Spiritual ambition in this dimension would include:

1. Preaching the Gospel to everyone within the limits of the distinctive ministry,

2. Rendering total obedience to the Lord, staying within His perfect will, and ensuring that the total fruit desired by God is produced both in souls reached for Him and in the Church building.

Therefore, spiritual ambition will always include a knowledge of Jesus and serving Him.

KNOWING CHRIST AS PAUL'S SUPREME AMBITION

Paul sought the Lord. The preliminary revelation on the road to Damascus only made him want to know Him more and more. He yearned for Him. He desired the Lord. He had a hunger for Jesus which nothing but Jesus could satisfy. He had abundance of revelation, but he still wanted Jesus. He sought Him in prayer, in meditation, etc. He read His word. Like the psalmist, he panted after the Lord. His desire for Christ could have been expressed in the following words:

"*O God, thou art my God, I seek thee, my soul thirsts for thee; my flesh faints for thee, as in a dry and weary land where no water is. So I have looked upon thee in the sanctuary, beholding thy power and glory. Because thy steadfast love is better than life, my lips will praise thee*" (Psalm 63:1-3).

So intense was Paul's desire for the Lord that he desired to depart out of this life so as to go and be with Him. He said, "*My desire is to depart and be with Christ, for that is far better*" (Philippians 1:23).

KNOWING THE POWER OF THE RESURRECTION

The power of the resurrection, which is the power that brought Jesus back to life from the dead, is nothing else besides the power of the Holy Spirit. Paul had spiritual power. He performed many miracles by the power of the Holy Spirit. People praised him and some wanted to worship him. He himself testified to the fact that his ministry was in great power. He said, "*For I will not venture to speak of anything except what Christ has wrought through me to win obedi-ence from the Gentiles, by word and deed, by the power of signs and wonders, by the power of the Holy Spirit so that from Jerusalem and as far round as Illyricum I have fully preached the gospel of Christ*" (Romans 15:18-19), and again, "*For our gospel came to you not only in word, but also in power and in the Holy Spirit and with full conviction*" (1 Thessalonians 1:5). In spite of all this experience of the power of the Holy Spirit, Paul was far from satisfied. He knew that more was in store. He knew that the Lord Jesus said, "*Truly, truly, I say to you, he who believes in me will also do the works that I do, and greater works than these will he do, because I go to the Father*" (John 14:12).

He ever sought these greater works which Jesus promised; for he well knew that the promise was meant to be realized. Therefore, he did not sit down, relax, and congratulate himself. Rather, he did all that was possible to enable him to know in experience all of the Holy Spirit. He had not yet arrived, but he was working at it all the time.

KNOWING FELLOWSHIP WITH CHRIST IN HIS SUFFERING

Paul suffered enormously for the gospel. He summed up his suffering in the following words: "*Five times I have received at the hands of the Jews the forty lashes less one. Three times I have been beaten with rods; once I was stoned. Three times I have been shipwrecked; a night and a day I have been adrift at sea; on frequent journeys, in danger from rivers, danger from robbers, danger from my own people, danger from Gentiles, danger in the city, danger in the wilderness, danger at sea, danger from false brethren, in toil and hardship, through many a sleepless night, in hunger and thirst, often without food, in cold and exposure*" (2 Corinthians 11:24-27).

One would normally have said: "He has had enough. He should run away from suffering." However, Paul did not think that way. He estimated that his suffering was very little compared to his Lord's, and so he had a desire to know in an increasing and finally in a supreme way, fellowship with the Lord in His suffering.

Why did he want more suffering with the Lord? He knew that suffering was the pathway to glory for the Lord. The Bible says, "*For it was fitting that he, for whom and by whom all things exist, in bringing many sons to glory, should make the pioneer of their salvation perfect through suffering*" (Hebrews 2: 10). As a disciple, he knew that the more he suffered, the more he would better conform to His Lord. That desire to know fellowship with Christ in His suffering was more than fulfilled for him; for he died for the cause of the gospel of Christ.

KNOWING FELLOWSHIP WITH CHRIST IN HIS DEATH

Suffering for the Lord Jesus ended in death, death on the cross. Paul wanted to know fellowship with Christ in his death. He wanted to conform to Christ in His death. To some extent he knew this conformity as a daily experience. He said, "*I die every day*" (1 Corinthians 15:31). This daily dying continued until that day when he laid down his life for the Lord he loved so well.

KNOWING CONFORMITY TO CHRIST IN HIS RESURRECTION

The apostle Paul said, "*... that if possible I may attain the resurrection from the dead*" (Philippians 3:11). Paul knew that the Lord Jesus did not only die, but He also rose from the dead. He also knew that when the Lord resurrected there was a limitlessness in Him which had not been there before. He further knew that the believers would show forth the power and the glory of the Lord after the resurrection in a measure which they did not show forth then, even where consecration was complete. He also knew that the resurrection brought with it a resurrection body that was redeemed as it is written, "*We ourselves, who have the first fruits of the spirit, groan inwardly as we wait for adoption as sons, the redemption of our bodies*" (Romans 8:23). So in yearning that he might attain unto the resurrection from the dead, Paul was desiring that the following should take place in him, if possible:

1. Body limitlessness.
2. A resurrection body.
3. A foretaste of the power of the age to come.

Were these right desires? I believe that they were; for they came from a heart that loved the Lord deeply, and what can a lover not ask of the Beloved?

KNOWING CONFORMITY TO CHRIST IN CHARACTER

The character of Christ was perfect. There were no loopholes anywhere. He was the perfection of love, peace, patience, etc.

Paul wanted this. His desire was that when people saw him, they would see Christ. So he thoroughly imitated Christ. He put on Christ in the fullness of His character, yet even there he had not yet reached perfection. There was room for more growth, and that was why he made it his ambition.

Paul could not help desiring this conformity. He told his spiritual children to imitate him (Philippians 3:17). Could he have asked them to imitate him if his character and his sermons preached different messages? To have asked people to imitate him suggests that he had made much progress in Christlikeness. He had indeed gone a long way in the formation of Christ within. However, he saw that there was room for more progress, and that was why he yearned for greater conformity to Christ in the hope that he might be able to attain that perfect conformity to Christ which fully satisfies God's heart.

KNOWING A HOLY JEALOUSY FOR GOD AND A HOLY HATRED FOR THE WICKED ONE

Paul already made much progress in this realm of a holy jealousy for God's glory and a holy hatred for the wicked one. He manifested this by ensuring that the Lord had all that he was and all that he had. He laboured to ensure that, like in his Master, the prince of this world could come but not have nothing in him. Serious "lines" were drawn in his heart that kept the devil out. Wherever he saw the works of the wicked one, he destroyed them. He came into conflict with the Enemy ever so often; for he could not endure the fact that Satan kept in captivity blood-bought men who ought to be free.

He went very far in this area, too, but he had not yet reached the apex of perfection. As his knowledge of the Lord grew, so did his hatred for the devil. His hatred for the devil drove him to labour toward the liberation of all men from his illegal clutches.

SPIRITUAL AMBITION AND SERVING CHRIST

We have already said that Paul received a distinctive ministry from the Lord Jesus. He set out to serve Christ and thereby accomplish his ministry. In this area of spiritual ambition, we shall look at two aspects: the preaching of Christ and the building of the Church.

The preaching of Christ

Seven reasons at least can be given for Paul making the preaching of Christ the ambition of his life:

1. The call of Christ.
2. A sense of compulsion.
3. A debt to all men.
4. Necessity laid on him.
5. The blood of men.
6. The wrath of God.
7. The love of Christ.

1. The call of Christ

The Lord Jesus called Paul to preach the gospel to the Gentiles. It is as if the Lord said to him, "Paul, do one thing for Me. Preach My gospel to the Gentiles." That was all. Paul understood it. It was a command from the Lord. He had no choice but to fulfil it. Before then he was free, but from the moment he received that commission, he lost his liberty to do any other thing but that to which he was called.

2. A sense of compulsion

Having been called and commissioned by the Lord, Paul felt and knew a sense of compulsion characterised by the word "eager." He said, "*I am eager to preach the gospel to you also who are in Rome*" (Romans 1:15). The gospel was burning in his heart and he could not keep quiet.

3. A debt to all men

Within the limits of God's call on him, Paul said, "*I am under obligation both to Greeks and to Barbarians, both to the wise and to the foolish*" (Romans 1:14). Paul was sent to these people with the gospel. He had the gospel. They had nothing. He owed them the gospel. They owed him nothing. His debt was to all the Gentiles. He owed the civilised Gentiles, the primitive Gentiles, the wise Gentiles, the foolish Gentiles. Regardless of the social, academic, financial, moral, religious, or other condition of the Gentiles, the call made him a debtor to all of them. His preference for some class of Gentiles did not come in. Their looks were not allowed to interfere. Their attitude to him was not allowed to have anything to do with it. If they loved him, he was a debtor to them. If they hated him, he remained a debtor to them. It was a debt that forced him into action. He did everything possible for them.

4. Necessity laid on him

Because of the call of God on Paul, he could say, "*For if I preach the gospel, that gives me no ground for boasting. For necessity is laid upon me. Woe to me if I do not preach the gospel! For if I do this of my own will, I have a reward; but if not of my own will, I am entrusted with a commission*" (1 Corinthians 9:16-17). Whether Paul liked it or not, he was under duty, as an officer commissioned by Christ, to preach the gospel. The Lord Jesus, as Commander-in-chief of the army of God, called officer Paul and said to him, "Preach My gospel." Paul's feelings were then put aside. Only one way was opened for him if he wanted to remain in the army the way of obedience. If he did not obey, he was under a curse. He could not disobey and remain in the army. He could not disobey and not be cursed. It is as if a curse was already hanging on him and he could only get rid of it by preaching the gospel.

5. The blood of men

Paul was very versed in the Old Testament Scripture. He knew that God had said in it, "*I have made you a watchman for the house of Israel, whenever you hear a word from my mouth, you shall give them warning from me. If I say to the wicked, 'You shall surely die,' and you give him no warning, nor speak to warn the wicked from his evil way, in order to save his life, that wicked man shall die in his iniquity; but his blood I will require at your hand. But if you warn the wicked and he does not turn from his wickedness, or from his wicked way, he shall die in his iniquity but you will have saved your life'*" (Ezekiel 3:18-19). Paul knew the following:

a. All who did not hear the gospel must perish because of their sin, irrespective of whether or not they heard the gospel.

b. If the wicked were warned but they did not repent, he, Paul, was free from the wrath of God.

c. If the wicked were not warned, then he, Paul, would carry the blood of those wicked ones on his head.

d. The only way for him to be free from the blood of men was to preach the gospel to all the men to whom Christ had sent him. For that reason he put everything into it.

6. The wrath of God

Paul taught: "*The wrath of God is revealed from heaven against all ungodliness and wickedness of men who by their wickedness sup-press the truth*" (Romans 1:18). He further proclaimed: "*The unrighteous will not inherit the kingdom of God*" (1 Corinthians 6:9). Kno-wing this consequence of unbelief and the tragedy of hell, he committed himself to persuading men to flee the wrath of God. How could he rest when multitudes of sinners were still without Christ? How could he rest with multitudes on the way to the lake of fire? He could not.

7. The love of Christ

The seventh and the greatest reason why Paul was compelled to preach the gospel was the love of God. He knew that God loved the world and manifested that love by the death and resurrection of Christ. He knew the exceeding greatness of that love towards the most undeserving of men like himself. The gospel was good news, exciting news. It gripped the totality of his person, gave him the one reason for living, offered hope to hopeless men, and brought in a new day of God's grace in the place of His wrath. How could he let people perish in sin when such a remedy was available? How could he keep his mouth shut? The very content of the gospel for-ced him to do all to announce it.

These were Paul's reasons for preaching the gospel.

The Building of the Church

The building of the church of God was linked to preaching the gospel. All who responded to the gospel became a part of the church. He built the church:

1. Out of response to the call of Christ.

2. Out of a debt to the people he led to Christ. He felt compelled to labour until Christ was formed in them.

3. Out of fear lest they should backslide and fall away.

4. Out of a desire to co-operate with the One who said: "I will build My church."

5. Out of a desire to see the Bride of Christ established:

   a) without spot of sin,

   b) without blemish of distorted character, and

   c) without wrinkle of age resulting in the loss of the first love.

WHAT DID PAUL DO TO ENSURE THAT HIS AMBITION WAS ACCOMPLISHED?

He accomplished that goal by ensuring the following:

1. By having God totally on his side, by ensuring that he was totally on God's side.

2. By hard work. He was not lazy. He said, "*With far greater labours*" (2 Corinthians 11:23) and "*I worked harder than them all*" (1 Corinthians 15:10). Others worked, but he worked harder than them all. Part of his success lay in the hard work he accomplished. Had he been lazy, he would not have gone far. He was not only hard-working, he was very hard working. He allowed no time for leisure.

He was possessed and monopolised by God and was totally for God. He did not only tell the gospel, he did all in his power to send it forth.

3. He kept at his goal. He did not move to easier things when the going was rough. He had no choice. He was a slave of Jesus and so had only one direction opened to him. By receiving Jesus' call he lost all rights to personal freedom.

4. He identified obstacles and hindrances and forced them out of the way.

5. By extreme zeal. He had been extremely zealous pursuing dead works as a Pharisee. He had spent and was spent for what he later discovered as useless for him. Then he found the Lord the truth. No doubt his zeal overabounded. He burnt himself out in service. He was red-hot for God all the time.

6. He did not get things mixed up. He maintained the right sense of priority. He gave himself to what was most urgent and most significant by its impact on the Church.

7. He discerned the right time and moved in it. He also laboured to save time. He did not do in two minutes what could have been done in one minute. He knew that time was a precious gift from God and that the gift was perishable. He was all too sure that time was the one thing that could not be stored. He found that once it was lost, it was lost for ever. He then sought to use it as best as the Lord guided him, knowing that he would meet every day, hour, minute, and second at the judgment seat of Christ to give an account of how it was spent.

8. He selected the right co-workers, trained them, and gave them the opportunity to expand the work and thus serve the Lord.

He multiplied himself by producing producers of men!

9. He became anything for all men that he might win some. He himself said, "*For though I am free from all men I have made myself a slave to all, that I might win the more. To the Jews I became as a Jew, in order to win the Jews; to those under the law I became as one under the law though not being myself under the law that I might win those under the law. To those outside the law, I became as one outside the law not being without the law toward God but under the law of Christ that I might win those outside the law. To the weak I became weak, that I might also win the weak. I have become all things to all men, that I might by all means save some*" (1 Corinthians 9:19-22). He did everything that could be rightly done for the sake of winning some to Christ.

10. He used divine weapons and divine methods. He testified, "*For though we live in the world we are not carrying out a worldly war, for the weapons of our warfare are not worldly but have divine power to destroy strongholds*" (2 Corinthians 10:3-4).

11. He was prepared to pay the supreme price. He said, "*I do not account my life of any value nor as precious to myself, if only I may accomplish my course and the ministry which I received from the Lord Jesus, to testify to the gospel of the grace of God*" (Acts 20:24). "I am ready not only to be imprisoned but even to die at Jerusalem for the name of the Lord Jesus" (Acts 21-13).

12. He proclaimed the whole counsel of God. He did not preach the gospel in bits. He did not leave out the sharp edges so that it might be accepted easily. He preached all of it warning and exhorting men in all sincerity.

So he laboured to bring all men to repentance, to proclaim all truths of the word both the popular and the unpopular and laboured to bring each saint to maturity.

13. He put everything into it. He gave all of himself to it. It was total conflict and he was at it all the time. He pressed on, he strained, he strove and he won.

It was a victorious Paul who said before he died, "*I am already on the point of being sacrificed; the time of my departure has come. I have fought the good fight. I have finished the race, I have kept the faith. Henceforth there is laid up for me the crown of righteousness, which the Lord, the righteous judge, will award to me on that day, and not only to me but also to all who have loved his appearing*" (2 Timothy 4:6-8).

He started with a goal received from the Lord. Accomplishing that goal became the one ambition of his life. He had received instruc-tions from the Lord at the beginning and received further instructions along the way. He kept at his goal and refused to be sidetracked. He paid the price, finished his course, qualified for the crown and passed into the presence of the Lord he served.

Glory be to the Lord!

CHAPTER 5

THE GREATEST NEED OF THE HOUR

I believe that this is the most critical hour in the spiritual time-table of this nation, this continent, and this world. The Lord has put a message on my heart and I feel compelled to share it with you.

THE SUPREME COMMAND

The Lord Jesus said, "*All authority in heaven and on earth has been given to me. Go, therefore, and make disciples of all nations, baptizing them in the name of the Father and of the Son and of the Holy Spirit, teaching them to observe all that I have commanded you; and Io, I am with you always, to the close of the age*" (Matthew 28:18-20).

He again said, "*Go into all the world and preach the gospel to the whole creation. He who believes and is baptized will be saved; but he who does not believe will be condemned*" (Mark 16:15-16).

He again said, "*And this gospel of the kingdom will be preached throughout the whole world, as a testimony to all nations; and then the end will come*" (Matthew 24:14).

The Lord meant that this command should be obeyed. In a sense, it is His greatest command; for all His plans for all men are bound up in it. The early disciples obeyed it. Paul, for example, separated the disciples from the Jewish religionists, and within a period of two years all the residents of Asia heard the word of the Lord, both Jews and Greeks (Acts 19:8-10). The disciples in Jerusalem filled the whole town with the teaching of the Lord. The religious leaders said, "*We strictly charged you not to teach in this name, yet here you have filled Jerusalem with your teaching*" (Acts 5:28). "*Now those who were scattered went about preaching the word. Philip went down to a city of Samaria and proclaimed to them the Christ. And the multitudes with one accord gave heed to what was said by Philip*" (Acts 8:4-6).

These early disciples treated the command with the importance that the Lord gave to it. They gave it their all. This was in a sense their one occupation their only occupation. They gave it their all time, energy, intelligence, and all. If they were tent-makers, their true profession was proclaiming the gospel. They made tents to pay the expenses involved in proclaiming Christ. They never gave their hearts to tent-making. They never dreamt of the day when they would be promoted in the tent-making industry. They dreamt about proclaiming the gospel, about filling the world with the Good News that Jesus saves and saves completely.

They knew that the gospel had to be preached throughout the whole world as a witness before the Lord Jesus would return. They did not spend time day-dreaming about the second coming and hair-splitting about details when most of the world had not yet heard of the First Coming.

They obeyed the Lord. They were disciples; for disciples obey the Lord in all things at all times. This was the Lord's foremost command, and they made it the one command that had to be obeyed before all the other ones.

They assessed their lives by one invariable standard, "Am I obeying the command to go into the world and make disciples of all nations?"

They did not deceive themselves. They faced facts the facts related to the making of disciples of all nations. If you are not actively obeying that command, you are disobedient and, consequently, outside God's will!

THE SUPREME BURDEN

There is a burden on God's heart. His burden is that the people whom His Son purchased by His death on the cross are yet lost in sin, not because they do not want to hear about Him, but because they have not been told about Him. He does not want anyone to perish. The Bible says, "*The Lord is not slow about his promise as some count slowness, but is forbearing toward you, not wishing that any should perish, but that all should reach repentance*" (2 Peter 3:9).

People at different times have caught the burden that God has.

Paul saw the vision of what God had in mind and also saw the lost condition of his tribesmen. He then said that he had unceasing sorrow, great anguish, and a heart's desire for the lost Jews whom he wanted to come to a saving knowledge of Christ. The burden weighed so much on him that he considered that he was under a curse if he did not preach the gospel. The early disciples so felt the burden of lost souls that they went everywhere preaching the gospel of the Lord.

God needs people whose burden for the lost is so great that they will not know one minute's joy while multitudes pass without Christ into the lake of fire.

THE SUPREME NEED: LABOURERS

The Lord Jesus saw the obvious need for labourers. He encouraged the disciples to pray for labourers. He said, "The harvest is plentiful, but the labourers are few; pray, therefore, the Lord of the harvest to send out labourers into his harvest" (Matthew 9:37-38). The harvest is His. Only He can send out labourers. There are three types of labourers needed by the Lord. He needs labourers who will:

1. Preach the gospel,
2. Intercede,
3. Give sacrificially.

Those who will live and preach the gospel are the ones who have died to the world, the flesh, and the devil and who, of consequence, cannot be trapped by the wicked one. These are people whose character has so undergone the purifying and perfecting work of God that God can depend on them to rightly represent Him.

He needs those who will intercede for the lost. He said, "*The people of the land have practised extortion and committed robbery; they have oppressed the poor and needy, and have extorted from the sojourner without redress. And I sought for a man among them who should build up the wall and stand in the breach before me for the land, that I should not destroy it but I found none. Therefore, I have poured out my indignation upon them; I have consumed them with the fire of my wrath; their way have I requited upon their heads; says the Lord God*" (Ezekiel 22:29-31). Here it was principally a divine need. Although the people deserved destruction, God out of love did not want to destroy them. He, however, could not just twist the demands of divine justice. Two things were possible. Someone either stood in the gap and interceded so that the people were spared, or they had what they deserved. Because God wanted to spare them, He Himself went out looking for one person who could stand in the gap so that they would be spared. He did not require two people just one but He did not find that one. So he reluctantly poured out His anger. What if He had found an intercessor? The people, though sinful, would have been spared so that they could have another chance to respond to the love of God. Because no intercessor was found, multitudes perished. Could it be that the sin of some particular nation, province, town, village, etc, has gone up continually to God but yet He wants to spare it if He could find an intercessor? Can you be counted upon to stand in the gap? Do you know the secret of standing in the gap? Do you know the authority of an intercessor? Are you able to satisfy this current need of God?

Where are those who can say to the Lord, "*For Zions (Cameroon, Africa, the world)'s sake I will not keep silent, and for Jerusalems sake I will not rest, until her vindication goes forth as brightness, and her salvation as a burning torch*"? (Isaiah 62:1). Can God say the following because you are available?

"*Upon your walls, O Jerusalem*

[Yaounde, Cameroon, Africa, the world]

I have set watchmen;

all the day and all the night

they shall never be silent.

You who put the Lord in remembrance

take no rest,

and give him no rest

until he establishes Jerusalem

[Yaounde, Cameroon, Africa, the world]

and makes it a praise in the earth" (Isaiah 62:6-7).

Others may be unavailable but can He at least say of you, "I have set a watchman?" Do you know something of taking no rest and giving Him no rest night and day as you labour in intercession? Have you ever interceded until all of your body was bathed in sweat?

The Enemy is attacking God's special property, the Church. Where are those able soldiers who can wage prayer warfare and carry out the following :

"*All nations surrounded me;*

in the name of the Lord I cut them off!

They surrounded me, surrounded me on every side; in the name of the Lord I cut them off!

They surrounded me like bees, they blazed like a fire of thorns; in the name of the Lord I cut them off!"? (Psalm 118:10-12).

Are there faithful intercessors to whom God can say the following?

"*Let the faithful exult in glory; let them sing for joy on their couches, let the high praises of God be in their throats and two-edged swords in their hands, to wreak vengeance on the nations and chastisement on the peoples, to bind their kings with chains and their nobles with fetters of iron, to execute on them the judgment written!*" (Psalm 149:5-9).

This is glory for all his faithful ones. Praise the Lord!

Will God find faithful men and women of prayer who will surround each aspect of the work with prayer and build prayer walls round each worker so that all attempts of the Enemy to destroy them are frustrated? This is God's greatest need at the moment.

The sad thing about it is that although this ministry of intercession is open to all the saints:

- the rich,
- the poor,
- the healthy (physically),
- the sick (physically),
- the educated,
- the uneducated,

- males,
- females,
- etc.

Yet it is the one where labourers are in the shortest supply. This surprises God. The Bible puts it bluntly: "*The Lord saw it, and it displeased him that there was no justice. He saw that there was no man, and wondered that there was no one to intervene*" (Isaiah 59:15-16).

God wondered! He was surprised! He was "shocked"! Must it repeat itself today?

God needs those who will give sacrificially. The truth is that the gospel enterprise needs funds. There is the need of producing tracts, booklets, books, Bibles, etc. There is the need to support those who cannot live by tent-making. The communists printed four pieces of separate literature for every human being in the world baby, adult, literate, illiterate, and all as far back as the year 1952. I do not know how many are being produced today. The number is certainly on the increase. Literature of the Bahai Faith is coming into our country at an enormous rate. There are hardly any Christian tracts that are well thought out, well produced and very presentable. The vision for tract production of the quality that communicates well to the African has been received. The few tracts that have gone into circulation have produced a rich harvest of souls for the Kingdom and created hunger in many for the Lord of life. However, the quantity produced is too small. All the other needs of the ministry that need finances are hindered by the low availability of funds. Is that right before God?

Ten francs can purchase one tract. The money for one bottle of soft drink can purchase twenty tracts. The price of one pair of trousers or one shirt can produce enough tracts to reach out to about one thousand people. Everyone can give to the work of the Lord.

Is it right to feed gluttonously while men perish without Christ for lack of funds?

Is it right to invest on much clothing when many have their sins not covered under the blood of the Lord because of the lack of funds?

Is it right to store bank deposits when men have no place where to hide from the wrath of God because of the ignorance of the supreme sacrifice on Golgotha?

Could the closing of your eyes to the financial needs of God's work be the reason for your spiritual bankruptcy?

Could it be that the Lord is talking to you in the following message?

"*Thus says the Lord of hosts: this people say the time has not yet come to rebuild the house of the Lord. Then the word of the Lord came by Haggai the prophet, 'Is it a time for you yourselves to dwell in your panelled houses, while this house lies in ruins? Now therefore thus says the Lord of hosts: Consider how you have fared. You have sown much, and harvested little, you eat but you never have enough; you drink, but you never have your fill; you clothe yourselves, but no one is warm, and he who earns wages earns wages to put them into a bag with holes. Thus says the Lord of hosts: Consider how you have fared. Go up to the hills and bring wood and build the house, that I may take pleasure in it and that I may appear in my glory, says the Lord. You have looked for much, and, lo, it came to little; and when you brought it home, I blew it away. Why? says the Lord of hosts. Because of my house that lies in ruins, while you busy yourselves each with his own house. Therefore, the heavens above you have withheld the dew, and the earth has withheld its produce. And I have called for a drought upon the land and the hills, upon the grain, the new wine, the oil, upon what the ground brings forth, upon men and cattle, and upon all their labours*" (Haggai 1:2-11).

People have not heard the gospel because believers are giving too little. It costs to send pioneer workers. Just the cost of transportation to mission fields and basic allowances for clothes and food excluding all luxury, amounts to considerable sums. Must people die without Christ while believers live in the comforts of an earth-bound people?

I shall never forget an event that happened some years in the past. I was carrying out an evangelistic campaign in one of the major towns of our country. Believers went out to witness in teams of two. The teams came back for evaluation. One team said: "We entered the house of a Moslem. The husband was not at home but the wife was willing to listen. We asked her if she knew Jesus at the personal level. She apologised and asked if Jesus was the name of a popular trader who had come to town. She confessed that she had not been to the market for a few weeks and was out of touch with the latest news!" This young woman was living in a Cameroonian town with a population of 50,000 people and she had never heard the name Jesus! At least she had not heard it enough to remember it! Why is that so? It is partly because believers give too little for evangelism and church planting. Where are those on whom God can count to supply the financial needs of His work?

THE SUPREME COST: SUPREME SACRIFICE

The greatest need of the hour is for people who will pay the price that is needed to do God's work, God's way.

1. There is an urgent need for crucified men to proclaim a crucified Saviour. (Self-seeking and sin-ridden men have monopolised evangelistic and other pulpits for too long. They are everywhere on the radio, television, newspapers, etc. They pat sinners on the back

and are interested in riches, honour, and all that the world that is hostile to Christ offers to sin-laden men). Oh that God would raise prophets!

2. God needs people whose lives are written off. Paul was one such man. He said, "*I do not count my life of any value nor as precious to myself . . .* " (Acts 20:24). Such men will proclaim the whole counsel of God and bear the consequences. They will not 'be found f? ting with kings, governors, and presidents. They will be hated men trouble-makers whose presence, like that of Elijah of old, will draw the following remark from royalty: "*Have you found me, 0 my enemy?*" (1 Kings 21:20). And they too, like Elijah, will not negotiate peace on sin. They will reply as he did, "*I have found you, because you have sold yourself to do what is evil in the sight of the Lord*" (1 Kings 21:20). They will not hesitate to pronounce judgment on a monarch who has deliber¬ately parted with God. They will say to him, "*Behold I, will bring evil upon you; I will utterly sweep you away, and will cut off from Ahab every male, bond or free, in Israel*" (1 Kings 21:24).

3. There is an urgent need for people who will give their lives and their all as Jesus gave His. He gave His all willingly. He held nothing back. He emptied Himself of all but love; yet hypocrites week after week raise voices of deceit to the Lord, singing:

Were the whole realm of nature mine

That were an offering far too small

Love so amazing so divine

Demands my life, my soul, my all.

Yet they sing ensuring that they do not give the little that they have. If a person cannot give God fifty thousand, how dare he think that he would give God the whole realm of nature if it were his? If God has given him fifty thousand to keep for Him and he hoards it, who will give him true riches of his own?

4. The widow gave her mite and satisfied the heart of God. She had nothing left that she could give. God is not as interested in what is given as He is in what is left behind. Solomon built a great temple for God. It was big. It was expensive, but did Solomon sacrifice for the Lord? No!

The temple was 60 x 20 x 30 cubits and was built in seven years. His own house was 200 x 50 x 30 cubits and was built in thirteen years. Such giving is worldly giving. Where is the sacrifice in it?

5. One woman broke her alabaster box of ointment and poured the contents on the Lord Jesus. Jesus said that she had done all that she could. In other words, the Lord was saying that she had done all that she could do. Where are young lives that are reck-lessly wasted on Jesus? Where are first class graduates, post graduates, a blessed people who will turn their backs on the world's folly and sacrifice themselves for the sake of the gospel of the One who gave His all? How can God be expected to manage with mediocres while the world is allowed to have the best talents?

6. Those who will win "the day" for Christ, like Paul, will know suffering. One of God's servants prayed, asking that God might move and turn whole continent to His Son. The Lord replied that He would do it but he would suffer more than his tongue could tell. Are there people to pay the price in the School of Utter Suffering and Rejection? How can people accept the mes¬sage of a rejected Christ from people who have never known rejection? Is it not normal that Christ, who was rejected, be represented and proclaimed by those who, like Him, have walked that same way?

THE SUPREME RESPONSIBILITY: THE BLOOD OF MEN

The Lord had promised to require from believers the blood of all those who have not heard the gospel. They will perish in their sins, but the Lord will turn to the believer and say: "Their blood is upon you." The extent to which you did not do all that you could do in full cooperation with the Holy Spirit to warn sinners of the conse¬quences of their sin, is the extent to which you are guilty of their blood. You are a murderer! Can you sit at ease when the blood of men is on you? That guilt so carelessly accumulated is the most terrible crime you can ever commit. To let a person die without Christ! Oh, Oh, how terrible! It would be better to send a dagger through his heart. It would be better to shoot him with a revolver rather than to let him die without Christ. Nothing could be one-millionth as bad as that!

Does the blood of the unevangelized not bother you? Does the promise of God that He will demand their blood from you look like a small matter? Will that alone not shake you out of your dangerous indifference and ease?

THE SUPREME URGENCY

There are many reasons why now is the only right time to act. It is the only time anyone really has to respond to the greatest need of the moment.

First of all, God says, "*Behold, now is the acceptable time; behold, now is the day of salvation*" (2 Corinthians 6:2). If the Lord says "now," and someone says "tomorrow," that one is an adversary of the Lord. All who change God's "now" into some other time are enemies of the Kingdom of God.

Secondly, it is urgent to get all the gospel out to all the world now because the doors may be closed. Ethiopia that was once open to the gospel is now a closed country. Communism has taken over. Angola is closed. This country could be the next to come under closed doors. Your country could be the next. There is no guarantee that the doors will remain open. Enemy forces are rising in great might and in great numbers. Communism is not the only enemy that could lead to closed doors. There is the force of militant Islam on the move and, worse still, the force of militant, impotent or pseudo-Christianity. There is no time to wait. Every minute lost is lost forever.

Thirdly, the harvest that is now ripe may be spoiled. There are a number of ways by which this could take place:

1. Softened hearts that are now ready may be hardened if not reached for the Lord. There is a limit to the time when softened hearts can remain open to the gospel. A day's delay can make all the difference.

2. Other doctrines may reach a hungry heart before the gospel of Christ reaches the ready soul. A person who is seeking God will open up to the first message about God that reaches him. What if the first message is the devil's lie? It could be a matter of hours and a soul is lost for all time and eternity. I once went to someone with the gospel. He told me, "You have come a bit too late. I have recently accepted one new religion that was introduced to me. I must find out all about it. I will not allow myself the confusion of facing two new religions." I was heartbroken. I had arrived too late!

3. Sinners may die without Christ. In as much as today is the day of salvation, today is also dying day. A sinner who is not reached today may be dead by tomorrow. Every minute is dying time. To say that you will only reach out to that person tomorrow may also

imply that he will never be reached at all. Death may reach him before the gospel.

4. The Lord may come suddenly. This is the time of grace. The Lord may come sooner than expected and all who do not know Him will be lost eternally. The Lord is coming. It could be tonight. Since the proclamation of the gospel is the most serious thing in all the world, is it fair to take the risk of pushing into the future what may be interrupted by the sound of the trumpet of God?

Finally, you, the one entrusted with the gospel, may be called home. Your life could end at any moment. No one has an absolute guarantee for tomorrow. This night the Lord of the harvest may sud-denly call you to give an account of the harvest that He has entrusted to you. If He wants something done today and you push it into the future for your convenience and then suddenly He says: "Procras¬tinator, come tonight and give account of your stewardship of souls," what would you say? Can you afford the tragic luxury of meeting the Lord with an unaccomplished commission?

These reasons and many others make proclaiming the gospel the most urgent thing on earth. There are things that can wait without serious consequences, but the gospel cannot wait. All waiting is fatal and beyond repair.

THE SUPREME GOAL:THE LOCAL AND THE INTERNATIONAL FIELD

The Lord Jesus said that the gospel was to go to all the nations. The whole world is included in the great commission. Those who are rooted in the ground may only see one individual or one place.

Those who rise higher with the Lord in the Spirit see whole villages.

Those who rise higher still see whole provinces and then entire nations and continents; and those who fly into the heights where the Lord moves see the whole world. God's vision is world vision. His harvest is world harvest. God belongs to all people and is interested in all men. He has no partisan spirit. Chickens can be partisan. They are on earth. Eagles cannot be partisan. They fly high.

Those who are faithful in witnessing to one person will be allowed to witness to other people. Those who are faithful in praying for one person and persisting in prayer until the person is saved will receive the capacity to pray for more. He who is faithful in a little will be given much to steward.

The best thing is to be faithful where you are. You will be given more in proportion to your faithfulness. The world may promote failures through corruption. God cannot be corrupted. He will not promote failures. Men can use the power of the dollar, television, etc, to give themselves a "World ministry." God has no part in it. He promotes those who pay the price and who pay it in its totality.

The supreme goal must be winning men to Christ and establishing them in Him. That is the only goal that will do. God will accept no other goals. That goal eliminates all other goals.

The supreme goal demands just one thing. The apostle Paul said: "*This one thing I do . . .* " He did not say: "These two things I do. "*Give yourself to the work of world evangelism. Be all that Christ saved you for and wants you to be. Venture for new places. The apostle Paul said, "Thus making it my ambition to preach the gospel, not where Christ has already been named, lest I build on another man's foundation, but as it is written: 'They shall see who have never been told of him, and they shall understand who have never heard of him'* " (Romans 15:20-21).

Paul set his heart on those who had never heard the gospel. He had not only the one ambition of preaching Christ but he wanted to be the first person to preach Christ to a certain people. He wanted to be a pioneer. He knew he would lay the right foundation. He was not so sure about the quality of foundations laid by too many people. He did not want mixtures.

There are still many places where Christ has not yet been named There are still whole tribes without a single individual's name from there in the Lamb's book of life. This is a most urgent need, for the Lord cannot return unless this happens. There must be people in the Kingdom from every tribe and tongue and people and nation. The Bible says, "*And they sang a new song, saying, 'Worthy art thou to take the scroll and to open its seals, for thou wast slain and by thy blood didst ransom men for God from every tribe and tongue and people and nation, and hast made them a kingdom and priests to our God, and they shall reign on earth'*" (Revelation 5:9-10).

May we repeat that this is the most urgent, the greatest need of the hour. God desperately needs those who will go where Christ has not yet been preached and has not yet been named. These kinds of places are the most difficult. They are the most challenging, but they provide the opportunity for dependence on God and the manifestation of the power of God as other situations do not.

There is a great need for apostles to go out today into these needy fields. I say that there is a need for apostles, but not for people of the average calibre of missionaries sent out today.

Most of them are spiritual babes and not apostles, yet they are expected to carry out apostolic duties! Many of them are spiritual dwarfs and not spiritual giants. Many of them are merely Bible School Graduates and not men of spiritual authority. Many of them are men of authority over funds and not men of authority over demons and evil spirits. Rarely do you find veteran evangelists among them, as many of them had never led five people to the Lord at home before they were sent out to the Third World. Many of them had never planted one church at home, but they are expected to supervise and direct the planting of churches in Africa, Asia, China, etc. Such babes will make the unreached tribes places for dangerous experi¬ments and not the establishment of the church of the First Born in splendour and in glory. The shortage of true apostles can never justify the sending out of babes for apostolic work.

The sad failure of most missionary enterprises through the send¬ing out of those men, men of immaturity, lacking in spiritual authority and experience, must not discourage anyone or blind anyone to the needs of those places where Christ has not yet been named. They are a top priority on God's list, and He is impatient to see them reached; so that His trumpet can sound and His Christ be revealed in splendour and glory.

God wants lives wasted on Him. He wants people who will pour out their lives as a libation on the altar of God's programme for the total evangelisation of the world. Such men will give their all to Christ, suffer the loss of all for Him, die possibly unknown to the mad world of religious play actors, leave hardly a franc behind as personal wealth, but win a coveted position in God's Hall of Fame. The question remains, "Will God find such men?"

They will have to be men of violence who take the Kingdom by violence as the Bible says, "*From the days of John the Baptist until now the kingdom of heaven has suffered violence and men of violence take it by force*" (Matthew 11.12). These people will be men of aggression, who can respond to a challenge. They will be men of authority before whom the powers of darkness find that they have no choice but to bow. They will have one attitude to all obstacles, be they human governments, religious organisations, denominations, or vari¬ous philosophies like: communism, humanism, consciencism, or indi¬viduals that stand in the way of their accomplishing God's eternal purpose. They will use the most powerful weapons of the power of prayer and the Holy Spirit to bring down these obstacles and destroy them completely. They will never resort to physical violence or force. They will war in the Spirit and in the Spirit alone.

Such men will accept no negotiations. They will state God's position and stand by it even at the cost of their lives.

Such men are the greatest need of the hour. May God raise them quickly! May all who know and love Him co-operate with Him so that He can find the right labourers for His harvest. Amen.

CHAPTER 6

SERVING THE LORD TODAY

Having read the "Distinctive Ministry," the Call of God in "Jesus Christ, God's Supreme Servant," "Spiritual Ambition as Exemplified in the Life of Paul," and "The Greatest Need of the Hour," someone may say in his heart: "I truly want to serve the Lord. How should I go about it?" In this part of our study, we shall try to face some of the practical issues involved in serving the Lord.

BEGIN BY SERVING IN THE LOCAL ASSEMBLY

The best place to begin serving the Lord today is in the local Assembly. Take your place in the Local Assembly. Submit to the leaders and serve the Lord in a general way as the Assembly does. Carry out practical work as well and don't only wait to preach. God is interested in all the work of the Assembly. In His mind, there is no division between spiritual and practical work. Be faithful in all that you do, for God will give you further ministry only if you are faithful in the general ministry.

RECOGNISE THAT THE HARVEST BELONGS TO GOD

The Father is the Lord of the harvest. The harvest is His. He appoints people and places them in various places in His harvest. Rest in Him. Do not seek your own will or your own way. There is no room for self-will in the service of the Lord. There are two basic requirements in the service of the Lord. The first one is sanctification. The second one is availability.

Separate yourself from all sin. Deal radically with all sins in your life. Do not sympathise with any sin whatsoever. Any sin you tolerate will eliminate you from divine service. God will not allow those who continue to practise sin to serve Him. He will look at your heart before He appoints you to any service. If your heart is impure, He will leave you aside. This condition cannot be negotiated. Do you want to be used by God in a lasting way? If your answer is "yes," you will prove your seriousness by offering to Him a clean vessel.

After you have purified your heart in the blood of Christ and have radically terminated with all sin, determine never to walk in the way of sin. You should do the second thing that is necessary: offer yourself to the Lord. Tell the Lord that you recognise the fact that you have no right to serve Him. Tell Him that you will be most grateful if He allows you to serve Him. Beg Him. Offer yourself to Him totally and without reserve. Tell Him that you do not come with any conditions to lay before Him. Tell Him that you will gladly do any job that He gives you.

WAIT ON THE LORD SO THAT HE MAY REVEAL HIS PERFECT WILL FOR YOUR LIFE TO YOU

There is a model in the heart of God for each life. God has already worked out in detail His perfect will for the life of each of His children. The Christian way is the way of discovering that model and living it out. God has a particular ministry prepared and reserved for you from the very foundation of the world. He has worked out what you should do every second of your life if you walk in His perfect will, and He has also established where you should be. There is a blueprint on each life.

God's perfect will for you is the best thing that can ever be designed for you. He worked out that will for your best interest in all time and in all eternity. It is a million times better than the best design that you can ever work out for yourself. In His perfect will you will satisfy Him. Outside His perfect will, you may still be blessed by Him, but you will never satisfy His heart.

Tell God that you would like to be part of the answer to the greatest need of the hour. Pay the price for being used in a mighty way. Seek the Lord and know Him very deeply. Do not be satisfied by the low-level Christianity all around you. To be used by Him in a distinctive and far-reaching way demands extra sacrifice. In this, God gives freedom to people. Those who seek Him the most and obey Him most unconditionally are given special privileges for service.

RECEIVE YOUR DISTINCTIVE MINISTRY FROM THE LORD

Ask the Lord to reveal to you the specific ministry which you are to receive from Him. Wait before Him in much prayer and fasting. This may go on for a long time. He will weigh your heart to see if you are sincere in your desire to serve Him. He will find out if your heart is liberated from material things, fame, the world, etc. He will find out if you are committed to obeying Him at any cost.

This process of weighing your heart may take some time. Sometimes God will be quiet for some time to see if you are bent on waiting on Him or if you will take things into your hands and go to carry out the desires of your heart.

As you wait on the Lord, ensure that your natural inclinations, prejudices, etc, do not come in. If they do come in, you may be led away by your own desires, thinking that it is God leading.

As you wait on God, He will make you know why He has called you. You may hear a voice speaking to you; and you may have a deep spiritual impression on your spirit or you may have a deep burden placed on your heart for a particular place or people. He may tell you to become a part of a ministry that He has given to someone. Whatever will be the way by which He will "talk" to you to communicate your ministry to you, one thing is certain: He will communicate with you. He has promised to guide you. He says, "*I will instruct you and teach you the way you should go; I will counsel you with my eye upon you*" (Psalm 32:8).

When God has spoken to you, it is best to ask Him to confirm what he has shown you through another member of the Body. This is very normal. He appeared to Paul on the way to Damascus and gave him a distinctive ministry, but he remained in the general service of the Lord until the Lord spoke through the church in Antioch.

Some people ask God for signs. Others, like Gideon, place fleeces before Him, while others, like the disciples before Pentecost, cast lots to ascertain God's will. I am not against any of these methods. God does indeed use them to guide young believers who have not yet known how to discern God's will by the peace of God ruling in their hearts. For the mature, these signs are unnecessary. The peace of God will umpire their lives so that when they are in the centre of God's will, that peace will rule perfectly, and when there is something wrong, that disturbed peace, like the umpire's whistle, will signal the fact that God wants to say something.

DISCERNING GOD'S TIME TO BEGIN THE DISTINCTIVE MINISTRY

From the moment that the Lord shows you what He has called you to do for Him, you must know for certain that the power of all other claims on you is finished. This does not, however, mean that you should set out at once in the way of your new distinctive ministry. God has the exact time at which you are to start. Do not rush on your own. The Lord called the twelve disciples to be with Him so that He might leave the Church in their hands. However, they needed three years of training. It may be like that for you. Moses spent forty years in the University of God. God will enrol you there and only send you out to your specific ministry when you have taken the Basic Courses and the Specialised Courses that are necessary for the work to which He has called you. The length of time you spend in His University will depend on how much work of the cross has already been carried out in you, and on your willingness to obey as soon as He speaks to you.

When your fundamental training is over, He will not wait too long before He sends you out. One thing that you should do during this time of preparation is to talk with God about the task to which He is calling you. Ask Him about the extent of the ministry and obtain from Him its limitation. Ask and receive from Him His methods for the work. Ask and receive from Him any co-labourers that He has in store for you. The crucial thing is that you receive instructions clearly and you discern them properly. There are some things that the Lord will not tell you from the beginning. He told Paul that he was to be a witness to the things that he had seen and the things that He was to show him later on. If you are used to dealing with God, you will easily discern what God wants to reveal to you and the things about which He would rather be silent. Do not force things out of Him.

RECEIVE A SUPREME BURDEN FOR THE MINISTRY GIVEN TO YOU

God may call you to things about which you may have no natural inclinations. He may send you to a people you naturally despise or to a people you know nothing about. He may send you to work in a ministry committed to the leadership of a brother you would naturally want to avoid. In addition to these instances, He might create in you a burden for a place or a person or a ministry. It must come from the Lord. Ask Him for it. In prayer, thank the Lord for the distinctive ministry that He has given to you. Tell Him that you have no burden for that ministry. Confess all the misgivings in your heart to Him. Do not pretentiously say that it is wonderful and give Him praise that has its origin only from your lips. Be honest with Him.

After you have said all that you want to say to Him, commit yourself afresh to Him and express your faith in His predetermined choices for you. Confess to Him that He is right, ask Him to give you such a burden for the ministry He has given you that will remain on you and grow in you until the ministry is accomplished. Having asked Him, you should not move away and just say that things are alright. Wait before Him and, if need be, continue to wait before Him. Sometimes it may be necessary to lie prostrate before Him for hours and days. When you decide to enter into such transactions with God, you are in for serious business and they take time. As you wait before Him in prayer, tears, agony, and rending of heart, He will do one thing: He will take your heart and weld it to the ministry He has given you, and then pour out the burden in His own heart for that ministry into your own heart. When that transaction is over, you will find that you do not need to make an effort to care for the place, person or ministry. You will find yourself caring and, as you walk with God, the burden will increase and a desire to have God's will accomplished in that ministry will burn within your being. Yes,

God lights a flame of love in the hearts of those who wait on Him for the ministry He gives them; so that they find the yoke light.

THE COST OF DISTINCTIVE MINISTRY

When God reveals to you that which He has called you to do for Him, He will want you to put all of yourself into it as well as all that you have. Your time, your energy, your thoughts, etc, are to go into it. Your ministry is to be the very reason for your life. You are to dream of it at night and work on it in the day. You are to work hard at it. You are to bury your best hours in it. You are to cry out to God so that He may give you all the wisdom that you need to make a success of it. You are to labour on it on your knees in prayer and by physical work. If men stand in your way, you are to pray them off. If you are confronted with a choice between obeying the dictates of men and the commands of God, you are to obey God rather than men.

THE PRICE OF DISTINCTIVE MINISTRY

From the moment when you receive a distinctive ministry from the Lord that has something to do with the salvation of sinners and their establishment in the Body of the Lord, the following become true of you:

1. You become a debtor to all men within the reach of your ministry, owing them the Lord Jesus and His glorious gospel.

2. There is a curse on you if you do not preach the gospel.

3. The blood of the men that God has granted unto you to lead to Him but whom you do not, is on you.

THE PROBLEM OF DISTINCTIVE MINISTRY:

1. Barrenness

Many people think that if a ministry is given by the Lord and the minister is in the centre of the will of God for his own life and the ministry, there will automatically be abundant fruit. This is not necessarily so. A ministry may be of the Lord, be carried out in the power of the Holy Spirit and in God's time, and yet not produce any immediate fruit. There are a number of reasons for this.

First of all, an ephemeral harvest that comes easily may not last. Lasting fruit takes time, and sometimes a lot of time, since it is to be watered sometimes by tears and sweat.

Secondly, that a work is in the centre of God's will does not exempt it from attacks by the wicked one. In fact, the more correct (before God) a work is, the more violent will be the attack of the wicked one on it.

Thirdly, God sometimes tests His servants to see their reason for serving Him. Sometimes He withholds the fruit to ensure that the secret motives of the heart are exposed. If someone is serving the Lord so as to obtain honour from men, he will need fruit very urgently in order to show his fans. If his only concern is the will of God, the glory of God and the interests of the Lord, then he will be glad to stand anywhere that the Lord puts him, provided the Lord is satisfied with him. After all, a servant is like a steward waiting on a master. All that he needs to do is to be clean and well-dressed, as well as available. If he satisfies all these conditions, but the master does not commission him to special duties but just allows him to stand by him at a table, apparently doing nothing, he is nevertheless fully occupied. He is on service.

2. Continuous Obedience

Sometimes it is easy to obey God from the beginning of the distinctive ministry, but afterwards it becomes very difficult to keep on obeying Him. Often the road becomes so much narrower with passing time that it is too much to continue on the pathway of obedience. Take, for example, Philip the evangelist. He was in Samaria. Things began to really move. He proclaimed Christ. Signs followed. Multitudes believed and were baptized, and there was much joy in the city. The apostles came from Jerusalem and the Samaritans were baptized into the Holy Spirit. Things were really going on well. Philip must certainly have been enjoying it. That was the type of place to stay in forever.

However, the Holy Spirit did not leave Philip there to establish the church. He did not leave him there to ensure that the church was well pastored. God saw that his ministry as an evangelist in Samaria was finished and He took him away! While everyone was enjoying all that was happening there, the Lord had other plans for Philip. The Bible says: "But an angel of the Lord said to Philip, 'Rise and go toward the south to the road that goes down from Jerusalem to Gaza. ' " This is a desert road. Had Philip not been fully surrendered; had he been seeking the glory of men, he would have tried to explain to the Lord, saying, "Is there some mistake somewhere? Am I supposed to leave this multitude in Samaria and go on a desert road? What does all this mean?"

However, he rose and went. He was obedient. Only the obedient can truly serve God in this way. As he obeyed, the Lord gave him another charge. The Spirit told him, "Go up and join this chariot." Again Philip obeyed. He asked no questions. He ran to the Ethiopian in the chariot, explained the gospel to him, led him to the Lord and baptized him with water.

As they came up out of the water, the Holy Spirit allowed no more contact between Philip and the eunuch; for the Bible says: "*And when they came up out of the water, the Spirit of the Lord caught up Philip; and the eunuch saw him no more, and went on his way rejoicing. But Philip was found at Azotus, and passing on he preached the gospel to all the towns till he came to Caesarea*" (Acts 8:39-40).

Philip was taken away by the Holy Spirit immediately he came out of the water. Why did God not allow further contact between him and the eunuch? Maybe the eunuch was planning to give him a sum of money that would establish him financially for the rest of his life, but at the expense of his ministry, and the Holy Spirit came in on time to ensure that this did not happen. Naturally thinking, Philip ought to have gone from Gaza back to Samaria. Was not that the place where God had used him in a distinctive way? Was that not the place where he had spiritual children who could stand behind his ministry in prayer and financially? Was that not the place he could make as his base? Common sense, natural logic, and all the tendencies of human security would have said: "Go back to Samaria. Protect your work from being destroyed. Establish your base." The Holy Spirit spoke and acted differently. He caught him up and he was now found at Azotus, and then on to all those towns until he came to Caesarea where he established a base.

When people receive distinctive ministries from the Lord, they must walk close to the Lord in order to discern when that ministry is over and God has something else in mind. God has mapped out how long each minister is to stay at a particular place and what he is to do while there. To fail to see this is folly.

All who serve the Lord must ensure that they stay within the boundaries of their ministries and that they do not build up monuments for themselves. They must move with God and stop with Him. If the Lord has used you to start a work, you should walk close to Him in order to know exactly when your part in that ministry is over, and you should leave in order to allow room for the next person whom God has ordained to continue from where you have left. Do not move away because there are problems which you cannot solve. Do not stay just because the work is going smoothly, the place is suitable for your health, and all the facilities you need to live like a junior minister in government are available. Move only because the Lord says "move" and stay only because the Lord says "stay. "Constantly remind yourself that the work belongs to the Lord. It does not belong to you. Leave the ultimate responsibility to Him. He knows what He is doing. He closes one door and He opens the other. Walk in dependence on Him.

EXPANDING THE MINISTRY WITHIN THE WILL OF GOD

How can the vision of the work to which God has called you expand? If the Lord first called you to win a town for Him, how can this expand to include other towns and possibly the whole nation, and maybe other nations?

The answer lies in revelation and the intimacy of the walk between you and God. Often, when God wants to do something, He looks for someone in whom He can confide. The Lord said, "*Shall I hide from Abraham what I am about to do, seeing that Abraham shall become a great and mighty nation, and all the nations of the earth shall bless themselves by him? No, for I have chosen him, that he may charge his children and his household after him to keep the way of the Lord by doing righteousness and justice; so that the Lord may bring to Abraham what he has promised him*" (Genesis 18:17-19). God had chosen Abraham for greatness, and so He could not hide what He was about to do from him. If you find favour with God, if you satisfy His heart through unreserved obedience, if your one ambition is to serve Him and have no other ambitions whatsoever, the Lord will reveal to you the greater ministry that He has in store for you. He will expand your ministry. He will give you new and greater fields of labour, and He will promote you. Many labour for the promotion that comes from boards boards of carnal men who know too little about prayer, waiting on God, and ministry in the Holy Spirit. These boards promote people to places of authority before men. The Lord promotes those who satisfy His heart. God's appointees satisfy Him and win a crown in the life to come. Men that boards appoint wear the crown of human glory in this life and that of divine disgrace in the life to come.

We repeat that if you are the right person, God will expand your ministry and reveal that expansion to you. He might have told you before, "Take this town for me." Now He will put a burden not only for that town, but also for other towns and perhaps the whole country on your spirit. You will then find that whereas before you were satisfied and at peace to pray the needs of that town through, that same ministry leaves you wanting more and more. You will begin to find that the Holy Spirit leads you to pray more and more for the new area, and the more you pray the more your spirit is united with the place, and inwardly you begin to find a sense of spiritual fulfilment. As you continue to pray, God begins to put a burden on your heart for the new area without taking away the burden of the first town that He gave you. This is expansion.

I must confess that it is difficult to communicate these transactions that take place in the human spirit. I can only clearly say that the Lord will expand your ministry if that is His will, provided that you have been faithful. He will make you know the extent of your new ministry, and He will place the whole territory, big as it may be, on your heart; so that you can truly bear it in prayer before Him.

As you pray and wait on Him, He will begin to grant you increasing revelation of what He wants you to do and how He wants you to do it. He will stand by you, give you fresh gifts for your expanded ministry, raise co-workers for you and, obviously, increase your joys and your sorrows. According to your faith it shall be done to you.

DISTINCTIVE MINISTRY IN SECRET

God may call you to a distinctive ministry of praying for some minister or some ministry. That, therefore, is a call to minister distinctively in secret. No one needs to know that to which the Lord has called you. There is no reason to publicise your ministry. You only have the duty to fulfil it.

In that kind of situation, He may give you the freedom to tell the person that God has called you to pray for him or He may tell you not to tell the person. One thing He will certainly do is that He will give you such profound love for that person and for the ministry that He has given that person to discharge that you will find a flow in the spirit towards him and towards his ministry. He will also put a special burden on your heart for the person and the ministry. That burden will be so clear and so heavy that you will feel like crying if you are not discharging it. You will find that the more you pray for the person and the ministry, the more the burden will increase and weigh on your heart. You should put everything into this kind of ministry as those in other ministries put into theirs. Praying for an hour or two a day cannot be considered as distinctive praying. It is general praying; for which saint can hope to make basic progress in the life of the spirit with less than an hour or two of praying every day?

So whole days or entire nights will be spent regularly in prayer. Sometimes long periods will be spent in prayer. It will be normal that a person who is called to such a ministry but who has to earn his bread from some kind of "tent-making" will withdraw during his leave periods of one or two or three months to a secluded place where all the time will be devoted to prayer and perhaps fasting.

Many people will not understand this kind of ministry. They will find it even more difficult to understand the withdrawal for long periods of prayer. They will not understand how God can call someone away to pray for many months. However, it is better to obey God than to satisfy men by obeying them.

It is even possible that the Lord raises people who will provide your basic needs and thus discharge you from the responsibility of making "tents" for a living; so that you can give your time in totality to prayer. This is something that will be sorted out between you and God as you go on.

DISTINCTIVE MINISTRY AND "FULL-TIME" WORK

Many people think that a distinctive ministry automatically means that the person is exempted from tent-making and lives on the funds of others and the churches. This must not be so. The Bible does not give us the picture of many people on whom the finances of the churches were spent because they worked for God all the time. The New Testament does not divide the servants of the Lord into two classes the full-time servants and the part-time servants. The Bible divides them into the faithful and the unfaithful.

We have proved in our own experience that a disciplined person whose heart is sold out to the Lord can use his day as follows:

1. 7 hours daily at his tent-making as demanded by the State,

2. 8 hours at the business of the Kingdom,
3. 9 hours for himself.

The thought that a person should be tired after seven hours at work bears testimony to an easy-going generation at the brink of economic, moral, and spiritual decay. In human history, real progress was made when people worked hard, sometimes more than fifteen hours a day. This worship of laziness and ease and its promotion in the name of the Lord lies partly at the root of the current spiritual and moral decay. Hard work will not kill anyone. If anything, it will help them to live long.

All the men whose lives and ministry were a great blessing to me worked very hard. None of them put in working hours that were less than fifteen hours each day. They caught the vision of God and they could not commit the crime of laziness. John Wesley, John Sung, Hudson Taylor, Pastor Tsi, Watchman Nee, etc, were men who knew how to make minutes count for the Kingdom.

I would personally not want to finance someone's food and clothing while he carries out some ministry unless he had demonstrated a real spirit of hard work. To be lazy in God's name is an abomination. Only when the person is already putting as much time into God's work as those people who are earning their own living and yet cannot complete the daily demands of his ministry should he be considered for support.

If an evangelist is not putting more than eight hours daily into the ministry, he should work and yet put in the eight hours because that is possible. Most campaigns are not carried out during working hours!

I understand that the locality may not permit working at tent-making and that may justify support. Well, such a person should justify the support by spending around sixteen hours in the ministry of waiting on God, prayer, Bible study, evangelism, edification, etc, daily in order to be considered faithful.

Again I insist that hard work is necessary. There are too many who are doing too little. The church is greatly hindered by indisciplined, disorganised, lazy, and purposeless leadership. This is a shame.

Again I suggest that before you consider leaving tent-making for some ministry where you will depend on others, make sure you are very hard-working and that you cannot with fifteen hours a day accomplish the work of earning your bread and the ministry that the Lord has given to you. If you live on the sacrifice of others or on the discipline of others while you yourself are not sacrificing your time and all for the Lord and are not disciplined, you are an unfaithful servant, and God will bring you to judgment. Think seriously about this.

I am quite convinced that those who exert themselves in the work of the Lord, who press on, who strain and strive, putting in every second of time and every ounce of energy, are easily recognised and no one can question their commitment. But alas, these are so few and their number is declining so rapidly that maybe in another ten years we will need to light a lamp in the day to try and find them if the Lord of the harvest tarries.

Are you hard-working? If not, there is a curse on you. Repent at once before you become a stumbling block to the Church. The Lord Jesus said, "*My Father is working still, and I am working*" (John 5:17). God has worked every second from the past eternal timelessness until the present, and will go on working without a second's rest in the future eternal timelessness. There is no substitute for imitating Him.

DISTINCTIVE MINISTRY AND FINANCES

There are many today who, while thinking that the Lord has called them to some distinctive ministry, nevertheless behave as if the One who called them to work for Him is not able to meet their needs. They, therefore, specialise in using underhanded methods to raise money for their work. This is very sad indeed.

When God calls a man to serve Him, the One who calls is respon-sible for providing the financial needs of that one whom He calls, as well as the finances of the work to which He has called him.

Moses did not discuss what his pay was going to be when the Lord called him. He simply accepted the call of God and went out in full assurance of the fact that the One who had called him was able and willing to meet all his personal needs and all the needs of the work to which He had called him. God did not fail him. He met all his needs and all the needs of the children of Israel, and all that was involved in moving out of Egypt into the Promised Land. The Lord did the same for all His servants in the Bible:

1. Isaiah
2. Jeremiah
3. Ezekiel
4. Daniel
5. Peter
6. John
7. Paul

None of these men ever asked God: "God, who will pay me? Who will pay the expenses of my ministry?" It was clear to them that the call by the Lord also included a commitment on God's own part to meet all the needs involved in the ministry which He initiated and called people to.

If the Lord has indeed called you to serve Him, you should entrust all personal and the ministry's financial needs on Him. If He cannot be counted upon to provide you with food and clothing, how will He then be trusted to give you souls for the Kingdom? It is possible to manipulate people to give you money, but whom will you manipulate to give lasting conversions and the formation of Christ in your converts? I strongly suggest that if you cannot trust God to meet your needs, you should not go out to serve Him because you will certainly fail.

I know of a brother who is the "Fund Raising Officer" of a large religious denomination. He told me that his job brings many conflicts into his heart; for when he visits the congregations on fund-raising trips, he often discerns the deep needs of the congregation but cannot minister to them in the areas of these needs, because a sermon that will minister to these spiritual needs may not be the type that produces immediate funds. I will never forget the agony on his face as he shared that with me. This is tragic!

It is best to leave the financial needs of the ministry and the ministers to the One who has called you to serve Him. If the Lord is truly at the centre of the work, He can cause funds to come in unadvertised. This will provide a good check; for if He is the Author of the funds, He will cause them to cease when the work has served His purpose, or when it no longer serves Him and He is forced to withdraw from it. This will be a blessing to the minister; for why should he waste his life in a work that no longer pleases his Master?

DISTINCTIVE MINISTRY AND MARRIAGE

Marriage is a most sacred union that can be dissolved only by death. Therefore, we recommend that it is better for a person to settle the call of God on his life before he gets entangled in the demands of the married life. A number of reasons make this recommendation prudent. First of all, the demands of the ministry to which the Lord will call you may make it necessary for you to remain unmarried for all or for some important part of your life; so that you can do a work for Him which will be impossible if you are married. If then you have gotten yourself yoked, you will find that you have eliminated yourself from God's best for you. Secondly, you may be married to someone who, though a believer, is not consecrated and, therefore, is unwilling to pay the price of pioneering work to which the Lord may call you. Therefore by rushing on to marriage you have eliminated yourself from God's best for you. Thirdly, the call of God on her life and the ministry to which the Lord calls you may so differ that you cannot work as a team. If you are already yoked together, the ministries will be greatly hindered or destroyed completely.

So, because of the prior claims of God on your life, ensure that a wife or husband does not come in to eliminate you from God's best for your life; for if you settle for the second best, you would have failed God utterly.

CO-LABOURING WITH GOD

The apostle Paul said, "*Working together with him ...*" (2 Corinthians 6:1). At the outset, it is God who called you and gave you a ministry to carry out for Him. What is the difference between working for Him and working with Him?

If you work for Him, you are on your own. He has given you a work to do and shown you how to do it. You then go on as best as you can. If, on the other hand, you are His co-worker, then the work remains His, the directives remain His. He is at the site of activity giving all the instructions and you cannot take one step independently of Him. If He wants the work to stop, it stops immediately.

Philip was a co-labourer with God. God was with him in Samaria. God moved him out of Samaria in the height of a great move of God in that city and he did not complain at all. God sent him to minister life to the Ethiopian eunuch, and just as that ministry was being completed, God called him away to another place. He had no plans of his own. He was not the captain. He was merely an assistant and he just did what the captain wanted done. When the captain said that it was time to move, he moved and did not worry about the work because the One whose work it was, was not worried about it. When the Lord called him away from Samaria, he did not complain as to what would happen to the converts. The Lord of the harvest owned the converts, and when He said, "move on," it was certain that He had other plans for them.

It is only in this sense of deep knowledge in real experience that the work, all of it, belongs to Him that there can be deep peace in the conflicts involved in the ministry. It is also in that sense that the work can remain God's work in every way and satisfy His heart.

My prayer for you is that God will truly open your eyes to see that you are only a co-labourer with Him, that all the work is His, and that because it is all His, you dare not bring motives and methods into it that will not fully satisfy Him.

This means that you will not expand the work beyond His limits for it or cause it to fail to reach the dimensions that He has in store for it. You will not try to impress men with numbers and buildings, etc. You will be content to please Him and not bother about the opinions of men. You will refuse to compromise anything or any truth so that the world may allow you to continue serving. You will walk close to Him, satisfy His heart, serve with Him, and win His "Well done, good and faithful servant," when He comes on that Day.

Glory be to His holy name!

CHAPTER 7

THE CHRISTIAN AND MONEY

THE CALL TO CONSECRATION

"*I beseech you, therefore, brethren, by the mercies of God, that you present your bodies as a living sacrifice, holy and acceptable to God, which is your spiritual worship. Do not be conformed to this world but be transformed by the renewal of your mind, that you may prove what is the will of God, what is good and acceptable, and perfect*" (Romans 12:1-2). I believe that this is the best place to begin this message on "The Christian and Money", because individual consecration to the Lord Jesus is the very basic requirement for any spiritual service whatsoever. We cannot sacrifice money to the Lord and His work if we ourselves are not sacrificed. If we are holding ourselves back or denying His Lordship in some area of our lives, then what we offer to Him of our material goods will count for nothing. God cannot accept a man's money when the man himself is not accepted by Him. God is not under obligation to accept any gift. If it comes from an unconverted or a converted but impure heart, He will reject it. It is said of the Macedonians that, " *... but first they gave themselves to the Lord, and unto us by the will of God*" (2 Corinthians 8:5). This principle of self being given first is again illustrated in the children of Israel as they left Egypt. They brought out with them their property gold, silver, cattle, etc. They could do this because they themselves came out of Egypt. It would have been unacceptable to the Lord if they had stayed in Egypt and yet deceived themselves into thinking that their property could go ahead of them and serve the Lord.

The supreme challenge of our time is the effective presentation of Jesus Christ as Saviour and Lord and the building up of the church which is His Bride. This is a difficult and demanding task. If we are to achieve our objectives, then a whole-hearted commitment is absolutely necessary. A young West African decided to become the Prime Minister of his country. This is how he thought about what it would cost him and how he must meet the cost. "*It will be understood that what I was doing was a complete volte-face in my personal habits. In my code of behaviour, even in my ethical and cultural standard, I could no longer be content with doing as much of what gave me pleasure as I could and as little of what caused me discomfort or boredom. The life before me was one of self-sacrifice and self-negation. I would have to give up many things which, innocent in themselves, might yet hinder the cause which was to become the purpose of living for me. I would have deliberately to judge my every action and decision by an invariable standard: Will it bring me any nearer my goal? In my dress, speech, and habits, I would have to proclaim my gospel, even though this might mean doing things in a way I might find inconvenient, and even distasteful.*"

If a non-christian said and did that to achieve his goal, ought not the children of the Kingdom do at least the same or more? Can a lesser standard of sacrifice be demanded of us?

THE CONSECRATION OF PROPERTY

At conversion, God puts His Holy Spirit within us. This sealing of the believer with the Holy Spirit constitutes a mark of ownership. This ownership is thorough. We become His servants, nay, His slaves, and we owe Him service. The Hebrew slave-owner also owned the property of his slaves. If our lives are consecrated to the Lord, then our property has to be consecrated as well. We cannot consecrate our lives and leave our property unconsecrated. Anyone who wants to follow the Lord and walk in fellowship with Him must bring all that he has and place it at the Lord's feet. He must bring all that he has and not just a part. Such property that has been given to the Lord in unconditional surrender becomes CONSECRATED property.

A two-fold deliverance

For the believer's property to thus serve the Lord, it must know a two-fold deliverance. First of all, it must be delivered from the world system; for money is part of the great world system that is hostile to God. The Lord Jesus called it "*The mammon of unrighteousness*" (Luke 16:9) and "the unrighteous mammon" (Luke 16:11). How is something that is basically of the world system, something that on its own is an enticement to sin, going to change and become of service in the Lord's Kingdom? There is one way the way of deliverance. The believer's property must be delivered from the world and its systems. At conversion when a person makes his exodus out of the kingdom of the Devil and is transferred to and born again into the glorious Kingdom of God's dear Son, he must bring all that is his along, out of the world into the Kingdom of the Lord. This means that the believer's property receives a divine touch. It is touched, as it were, with the blood of the Lamb who cleanses and sanctifies it. Secondly, it must be delivered from self. Many of the children of Israel left Egypt with property but they clung to it. They would not let it go into the Lord's service. It is possible for a believer to cling to things. If property is to become available to the Lord, it must be delivered from self: from that tyranny that wants to own it, control it and keep it for the use and worship of the god self. Therefore, the Holy Spirit must sever our property from the world and from self a two-fold deliverance. Such property that has been lost to the world and lost to self can be consecrated to the Lord. It can be offered to the Lord. All other property cannot be offered to the Lord.

Let us remind ourselves that it must be all. It is not just some percentage of the whole. If a believer does not consecrate all, then he can consecrate nothing at all. It is all or nothing! Let me put a question before each of us. "Has your money been delivered from the world and from self?" I do not know what your bank account is like or what you have in your wallet or all the property that you dare to own, but I ask you a simple question, "Has all of it been delivered from the world and from self and has it been consecrated to the Lord? Has it been offered to God in its entirety?"

It is sad to know that the wicked one has lots of money in his treasury with which to fulfil his purposes, whereas the Lord of glory appears to be poor because His children have much of their property under the devil's control.

God is not a rubbish heap

Week by week, the city council van comes to the place where we live and carries away a lot of rubbish. This rubbish is a collection of things that are useless to us or things that have become sour or are left-overs from meals. Some people, even God's dear children who have experienced the love that is ours because of His love poured out at Calvary, still make God a kind of rubbish heap. They give to Him the remains that are not useful to them anymore.

Others make God a kind of charity organisation. They give Him the things that they can spare; the things that they can part with without the slightest pain. This is all self-deception. It is not giving. In true giving, a person gives until it hurts to give. Have you ever felt, as you gave something to the Lord, that your whole being would break with that gift? If not, maybe you have never given at all.

God is not a beggar! God is not a charity organisation. He is the King of heaven. He is the King of all glory and He deserves the best. He deserves the totality of all that we have. It is His by right of creation. It is doubly His by right of redemption. This calls for a change of mind and attitude among many that are His children.

The right to use money

We have said that every child of God must consecrate all his money and property to the Lord. When this has been done, the Lord still makes us stewards of these things. He asks us to keep guard of these things for Him. We are to consecrate all that we have now and all that comes in week by week and month by month.

A faithful steward knows that he has no right to use his Master's goods without His expressed permission. The child of God has no right whatsoever to use any of his money or property without the Lord's expressed approval. He must ask for everything from the Lord. It is natural of man to ask God what he cannot get otherwise. It is in the spiritual man to ask and receive from the Lord that which he could otherwise have on his own. Let us take something very practical. Many say, "When I shall have saved a lot of money, I shall buy a house, an expensive dress," etc. Their problem is the lack of money at the moment. The child of God who has surrendered his all to the Lordship of the Lord Jesus will probably have a healthy bank account, yet he will not just use the money without permission. He will ask the Lord, "Lord, is it your will that I should build a house, buy a dress?" If the Lord answers, "Yes, you may buy a dress," then the obedient child can yet ask, "Lord, may I use some of your money to build the house, buy the house, buy the dress?" And a loving Father who approves of the owning of a dress will also approve of the money to be used to purchase it. This means that even the one without money in the bank can ask if he may buy a dress, and if the Lord approves the purchase, he will ask the Lord to provide the needed money from any source that He sees fit, and the Lord will do it. This brings all the surrendered disciples to the same level of possession, whether or not they have huge sums of money and property.

To go ahead and use "our" money without God's approval is to say very loudly that that money has never been delivered from self and has never been transferred into God's Kingdom.

This is a costly way of living, because it will mean that we spend time with the Lord in prayer asking Him to give us things that we could have bought on our own. But is this not part of being His slaves? It is also very costly because so much luxury, which is now characteristic even of true believers, will have to go! I think it can be said without room for much contradiction that a vast majority of the children of the Kingdom are worldly. They invest their lives as the world does! By their attitude to money, property, position, etc, they are saying that this matter of being a heavenly people sojourning in the world is a lie or at best, a theory. Brethren, let us examine our attitude to things: money and all that is associated with it and see if we are motivated for earthly gain. The apostle John wrote: "*Love not the world neither the things that are in the world. If any man love the world, the love of the Father is not in him. For all that is in the world, the lust of the flesh and the lust of the eyes, and the pride of life, is not of the Father but is of the world. And the world passes away, and the lust of it, but he who does the will of God abides for ever*" (1 John 2:15-17).

A world under judgment: lost treasures

The Lord Jesus said, "*Do not lay up for yourselves treasures on earth, where moth and rust consume and where thieves break in and steal, but lay up for yourselves treasures in heaven, where neither moth nor rust consumes and where thieves do not break in and steal. For where your treasure is, there will your heart be also*" (Matthew 6:19-21). The world was judged on the Cross as well as her prince. The Lord Jesus proclaimed it when he said, "*Now is the judgment of this world, now shall the ruler of this world be cast out*" (John 12:31). The world was not only judged; it was condemned. It has no future whatsoever. This has serious implications for the believer. He cannot truly invest in this world. He must not put anything of real worth into the world; for he will lose it. The world is like a bank that has been declared bankrupt. Take, for example, our national bank. If you were told today that it has gone bankrupt, what would you do? Would you deposit your money there anymore? If you did, you would be acting most foolishly, for all such money would be lost permanently. What a wise person would do would be to try and withdraw any deposits he has left in the bankrupt bank.

I warn all believers that the Lord's commands must be taken seriously. All permanent investments here must stop at once. We must cultivate and maintain a pilgrim's attitude to all that concerns the world. Every child of God must develop and maintain a deep seated disdain and disinterestedness in the world's love of money, fame, etc.

Lasting treasures

If the world is under judgment and is, therefore, the wrong place for the believer's permanent investment, what then must the believer do? Must he be lazy and, therefore, acquire nothing that is worthy to be invested? No. By no means. The believer must work hard and work intelligently. He must acquire wealth and he must invest it in heaven. Treasures stored there will last. They are indestructible. All believers must have treasures there. The sons of this world are busy laying up treasures in their destructible world and they are doing it whole-heartedly and at any cost. The Lord recommended this. The Bible says about the unjust steward: "*The master commended the dishonest steward for his shrewdness; for the sons of the world are more shrewd in dealing with their own generation than the sons of light. And I tell you, make friends for yourselves by means of unrighteous mammon, so that when it fails they may receive you into the eternal ha-*

bitation" (Luke 16:8-9). Money will ultimately fail when the Lord has brought this era to a close. However, at the moment it could be stored in heaven exchanged into the foreign currency of heaven and stored safely in the bank of heaven. That acquisition of money and the subsequent exchange and transfer into the bank of heaven must be done now; for soon it may be too late.

How can one convert, say, Cameroon francs or any local currency: sterling, dollar, etc, which are all earthly and perishable into the imperishable currency of heaven? This is accomplished by giving to the Lord and giving for the Gospel.

GIVING TO THE LORD AND THE LORD'S WORK

Giving unto the Lord was carried out in the Old Testament almost close to the very origin of man. Cain and Abel knew instinctively that they should give to the Lord. They both did. Later on, Abraham met Melchizedek. The Word of God says, "*And Melchizedek, King of Salem brought out bread and wine; he was priest of God Most High. And he blessed him and said, 'Blessed be Abram by God Most High, maker of heaven and earth; and blessed be God Most High, who has delivered your enemies into your hand.' And Abraham gave him a tenth of everything*" (Genesis 14:18-20). Melchizedek first brought out bread and wine and then he blessed Abram. He took the initiative. He gave and gave. Abraham responded and gave. Melchizedek is a type of Christ.

God is always the first Giver. He has given us Christ and every good thing. Our giving is only a response to His giving. It is a token of gratitude from those who have received their all from Him.

Abraham did not only give a tithe. He went ahead and offered his beloved and only son Isaac to God. Isaac symbolised all that he was and all that he had, and he gave Him away to God, holding nothing back. Yes, he gave a tithe but the tithe was followed by his all. The tithe was good but his all satisfied the heart of God and, in response to that offer, the Lord said, "*By myself I have sworn, says the Lord, because you have done this and have not withheld your son, your only son, I will indeed bless you, and I will multiply your descendants as the stars of heaven and as the sand which is on the seashore*" (Genesis 22:16-17).

The whole story is wonderful. God gave to Abraham freely. Abraham responded by giving a tithe. God blessed him even more by giving him a son and he responded by giving God his all. To this God responded by giving to him in a totally limitless way. Glory be to the Lord Most High! We, too, are called into this type of blessed relationship.

At the beginning of Jacob's walk with God, he said, "*If God will be with me, and will keep me in this way that I go, and will give me bread to eat and clothing to wear, so that I come again to my fathers house in peace, then the Lord shall be my God, and this stone, which I have set up for a pillar, shall be God's house; and, of all that thou givest me I will give the tenth to thee*" (Genesis 28:20-22). He was at this point in his pilgrimage just a carnal believer. He was a beginner, full of conditions. "If, if, if" He was carnal and calculating he would give 10 percent. Mathematical tithing is the business of carnal believers, of spiritual babes. The spiritual believer gives and gives and gives his all.

Jacob did not remain the mathematical giver. He grew. He sacrificed unto the Lord without bargain. The Bible says, "*And Jacob set up a pillar in the place where he had spoken with him, a pillar of stone, and he poured out a drink offering on it, and poured oil on it*" (Genesis 35:14).

When God desired that the tabernacle should be built, he asked that an offering should be taken for Him from every man whose heart made him willing. The offering was to be used for the tabernacle, but God considered it an offering for Him and He demanded that it be from people whose heart made them willing. God is too self-sufficient to compel anyone. He is too rich to beg. In the Old Testament the children of Israel gave tithes and offerings. They began with the tithe the place of law and mathematical giving and then they went into all types of offerings which were dependent on their love for God and their spiritual progress. As God continued to deal with His people, we find in the early church not one insistence on tithes but on offerings of love. It is no more law but grace. Grace finds the demands of the law superficial, inadequate. No one can live in grace and be satisfied to tithe. The children of grace give and give.

GIVING IN THE COVENANT OF LOVE

Jesus the supreme example

The apostle Peter said, "*For to this you have been called, because Christ also suffered for you, leaving you an example, that you should follow in his steps*" (1 Peter 2:21). He is our example in giving. How did He give? The Bible says, "*For you know the grace of our Lord Jesus Christ, that though he was rich, yet for your sake he became poor, so that by his poverty you might become rich*" (2 Corinthians 8:9). Christ gave His all not as a purposeless sacrifice but to make us rich. Believers are to give their all so that others may be made rich. They are to give away their riches and become poor so that some that are poor may become rich.

How Much to Give

We have said that the Lord Jesus gave His all and became poor for our sake. We are to give in the same way and to the same extent. Jesus gave all that God gave Him. The measure of our giving is the extent to which God has given to us. The apostle Paul says that we are to give as God has prospered us (1 Corinthians 16:2). Everything we have is a mark of God prospering us; so it must be available for giving away. Every time we give, our gift should cry out aloud, "This is the measure of God prospering me."

How to give

Settle with God beforehand what you are to give. Do not decide at the moment when the money is before you and you have pressures from left and right. The apostle Paul encourages us to put aside what we are to give long before the moment of giving arrives (1 Corinthians 16:2). Such giving is the result of a deep transaction with God, of a position reached with God after much heart-searching and prayer, and stuck to, regardless of other demands and changing circumstances. Please settle with God what you are to give and be sure that your gift satisfies God's heart. Do not wait to be coaxed by men's words. They may coax you to giving something to ease your conscience but it will never satisfy God. God loves cheerful givers (2 Corinthians 9:6-7).

My dear saint, does your giving satisfy the heart of God? Does your giving receive the commendation that you are a sacrificial giver? If not, your giving is a total failure and you will never move God's heart. God is not only concerned with what you give. He is even more concerned with what you have left behind for yourself. You may give hundreds of thousands but keep millions for yourself.

You are simply an idolater, a self-worshipper; for the object of worship receives the best share of everything.

May Solomon's example serve as a warning to us. He built a temple for the Lord. Its dimensions were 60 x 20 x 30 cubits and he put seven years into building it (1 Kings 6:2; 38). It all sounds wonderful but listen, he built his own house and its dimensions were 100 x 50 x 30 and he spent thirteen years building it! (1 Kings 7:12). The volume of God's house was 36.000 cubits and the volume of his own 150,000 cubits. God's house was less than 25 percent of the volume of his own house. He was in that sense an idolater. He later on worshipped at the shrine of idols (1 Kings 11:5-6) but this was only the product of a life of continued idolatry. He had already worshipped continuously at the shrine of the god of self!

The blessings of giving-1

The Lord Jesus said that it was more blessed to give than to receive. He also said, "*Give and it will be given to you*" (Luke 6: 38). How will it be given to you?

First of all, it will be given to you in good measure and, as if that is not enough, the good measure will be pressed down to create more room so that more good measure will be put in and, as if that were not enough, the pressed down good measure is shaken together in order that by being shaken together, room might be created for more. The room that is created by the shaking is again filled until some is running over (Luke 6:38). This is all wonderful. They are the promises of the unchanging God, and no believer should rest until he has put them to a test and found them to be true in an increasing and continuous way. This is God's pattern for the daily life of His children.

He further says, "*For the measure you give will be the measure you get back*" (Luke 6:38). This is the law of heaven. It says, "Give away and you will grow rich. "There is a contrary law the law of hell. It says, "Keep and you shall grow rich." We know that no one who does not give is ever really rich in the things that count.

This makes the quality of what we offer to the Lord become something of great significance. He will multiply what we give Him and give us back; so if we are to have the best, we must give Him the best. If we are to have much; we must give Him much. Take, for example, that the Lord multiplies what we give Him by a factor of 100. If I give Him 100 francs, He will give me 10,000. If I give Him 1000, I will receive 100,000. If I give Him 10,000 then I will receive 1,000,000. Giving to the Lord is a sowing process. You reap according to how much you sow and the quality of what your seeds are. The Lord Jesus gave His all and received all from the Father. The apostle Paul said, "*The point is this: he who sows sparingly will also reap sparingly, and he who sows bountifully will also reap bountifully*" (2 Corinthians 9:6).

Quality counts as well. The Lord Jesus gave His best and received God's best. If we sow our best, we shall receive I00 fold of God's best. If we sow left-overs, we shall receive a hundredfold of God's left-overs! Be careful what you give to God. Give Him the best, the topmost and you shall always have the topmost.

This, however, must not be allowed to degenerate into carnal bargaining. It is the flow of a yielding heart that is caught up with God and concerned only for God's interests with no selfish personal interests brought in. God will be preoccupied with the person who is totally preoccupied with Him.

The blessings of giving-2

When a person has truly begun to give and to give cheerfully, the following Scriptures will be applicable to that person. "*And God is able to provide you with every blessing in abundance so that you may always have enough of everything and may provide in abundance for every good work. 'As it is written, He scatters abroad, he gives to the poor; his righteousness endures for ever. He who supplies seed to the sower and bread for food will supply and multiply your resources and increase the harvest of your righteousness. You will be enriched in every way for great generosity, which through us will produce thanksgiving to God; for the rendering of his service not only supplies the wants of the saints but also overflows in many thanksgiving to God. Under the test of this service, you will glorify God by your obedience in acknowledging the gospel of Christ, and by the generosity of your contribution for them and for all others; while they long for you and pray for you because of the surpassing grace of God in you*'" (2 Corinthians 9:8-14).

First of all, God blesses in abundance so that those blessed may be able to give for every good work. God never blesses anyone so that he may hoard the riches. He blesses so that the blessings may flow out to others. Secondly, God is committed to supplying and mul-tiplying the resources of those who give. He is still the God of miracles. He multiplied the five loaves and two fishes. He wants to do that more and more, but His purpose is always that what is multiplied should be given out. Thirdly, giving is righteousness. When a person truly gives, he commits righteousness. Fourthly, giving results in an overflow of thanksgiving to God. Man is not the only one who benefits from true giving. God is also blessed. There is a twofold aspect to this:

1. The one who gives has a heart full of joy that results in praise and thanksgiving.

2. The one who receives is filled with joy that results in praise and thanksgiving to the Lord.

Lastly, giving is service. It is glorifying God. It is obedience.

The blessings of giving-3

God has promised to bless those who give. He says, "*Bring the full tithes into the storehouse, that there may be food in my house; and thereby put me to the test, says the Lord of hosts, if I will not open the windows of heaven for you and pour down for you an overflowing blessing. I will rebuke the devourer for you, so that it will not destroy the fruits of your soil; and your vine in the field shall not fail to bear, says the Lord of hosts*" (Malachi 3:10-11).

"*Honour the Lord with your substance and with the first fruits of your produce; then your barns will be filled with plenty, and your vats will be bursting with wine*" (Proverbs 3:9, 10). "*Riches and honour are with me, enduring wealth and prosperity. My fruit is better than gold, even fine gold, and my yield than choice silver. I walk in the way of righteousness, in the paths of justice, endowing with wealth those who love me and filling their treasuries*" (Proverbs 8:18-21).

The believer will be blessed as he gives. The blessing is the product of the giving and not the goal of the giving. The believer would still give whether or not God gave him back. He would give to satisfy the heart of God, but since God is all gracious, He will in turn give to the giving being.

Giving Out of Poverty

Many people mistakenly think that giving is a matter for the rich and the able. This is not true. Giving is for all the people of God, regardless of how much they possess. About the Macedonian church the apostle Paul said, "*We want you to know, brethren, about the grace of' God which has been shown in the churches of Macedonia, for in a severe test of affliction, their abundance of joy and their extreme poverty have overflowed in a wealth of liberality on their part. For they gave according to their means; as I can testify and beyond their means of their own free will*" (2 Corinthians 8:1-3). The widow who gave her last coins gave out of her need. She did not wait to have more. She gave what she had. She was in desperate need, yet she gave. She gave the last bit of her wealth. I believe that as her last farthings went away, that created a place for the Lord Jesus to take over in a very great way. She gave out of her need and she was blessed for it. May we learn from her. May we all learn to give in that way and then we shall receive the commendation of our Lord. "*Truly, I say to you, this poor widow has put in more than all those who are contributing to the treasury. For they all contributed out of their abundance; but she out of her poverty has put in everything she had, her whole living*" (Mark 12:43-44).

Begging to give

Many people think of a God who is in need and will of necessity accept just anything that is given to Him. This is very far from the truth. God has all that He needs. That He has "needs" that we can satisfy is only something that He has created in Himself out of love for us so that our gifts may have some place in Him. It is as if there is a self-created gap in Him which He waits upon us to satisfy. He is not compelled to keep the gap there because He created it not out of His own need but out of our own need. So giving to the Lord is for our own gain. Giving for His work is for our own gain.

When someone's eyes have been opened to what true giving is, such a person will beg to give. It is said that in western Uganda the subjects of the powerful Ankole Kings begged to give them gifts. A man would bring, say, three cows, prostrate before the king and say something like this, "Your unworthy servant has come to plead with you, that you may be so kind as to receive these three cows from his hands." The king would look away from the prostrating suppliant and say nothing, but his servant would tell the man, "Go in peace, the king has accepted your gift." The man would stand up and go away joyfully.

These people captured something of what giving ought to be. They captured it for an earthly monarch, but the church seems to have missed it for the King of kings. May God open our eyes!

In talking of the Macedonians the apostle Paul said, "*For they gave according to their means, as I can testify, and beyond their means, of their own free will, begging us earnestly for the favour of taking part in the relief of the saints*" (2 Corinthians 8:3-4). They begged for the favour of being allowed to give. They did not just beg, they begged earnestly!

Have you ever begged the Lord to receive a gift from you? Have you ever held your gift, prostrated yourself before Him, praying, begging, supplicating that He should grant you the favour of giving to Him? Have you ever begged earnestly, fearing that He could say no to you and then you would be undone?

Have you ever begged some servant of the Lord who has been given a special call and ministry from the Lord for the privilege of sharing in that ministry by your material and spiritual gifts? Have you ever begged to be given the favour of being a partner in some spiritual ministry being carried out by someone for the Lord?

Responsibility in giving

Every believer is responsible before God for the things that he supports and promotes. Should you support or promote things that dishonour Him, you shall suffer great loss on that Day the day of judgment of believers. Be very careful where you put your money, even the smallest sum of it. Discern everything prayerfully. Do not allow yourself to be carried away by the heavy advertisements of carnal people. Resist every attempt to be pressured by one or the other. Be moved only by the Spirit of God. The Lord has made you a steward of His riches. Never put them where he has not commanded you. Wait before Him. Do not just put in some money because others are putting in something. God will not be glorified by such giving. He accepts that which comes with joy out of a free spirit. He loves cheerful givers. He has no room for those who are pressured into giving. Many "pastors" who have fallen out of fellowship with God pressure people into giving. That is an abomination. They announce week after week that God loves a cheerful giver, whereas they really mean that they love cheerful (foolish?) givers, whose gifts will not satisfy the purposes of God but the tragic designs of men. Sometimes it is most painful to listen to these "commercial fund-raisers" who clothe themselves with Bible titles, but their motives and methods are eternally separated from God. Beware of them! I have had the sad dishonour of hearing them. They receive four, five, or more different offerings in one service. Their aim is to squeeze money out of men. God never does that. You will hear them say, "Now those who have ten thousand francs to give should come forward and give while all others wait." The carnal rich who have no treasures in heaven will come forward to display their carnal (earthly) wealth, knowing that they will have no reward in heaven and, therefore, must have some reward from men, here and now. After these, those with five thousand will come forward, and so forth, and, finally, the poor (who are possibly like the widow) will shamefully come with their five francs, mocked and disgraced by men but honoured by the Lord. Sometimes you will hear the fund-raisers say, "Search your pocket, please try. We will clap for anyone who comes to give now. Who wants to receive this special honour," etc. Then foolish men will respond. Sometimes the meeting places are turned into "Auction Blocks" to sell something whose actual worth is five hundred francs for five thousand! Others have finance cards where the gifts of the sons of the other kingdom are recorded for display so that those who so give can partake in the "communion."

All this is not of Christ. It is of the devil. No believer dare ever participate in such godless giving. The Lord Jesus said, "*Beware of practising your piety before men in order to be seen by them; for then you will have no reward from your Father who is in heaven. Thus, when you give alms, sound no trumpet before you, as the hypocrites do in the synagogues and in the streets, that they may be praised by men. Truly, I say to you, they have received their reward. But when you give alms do not let your left hand know what your right hand is doing so that your alms may be in secret and your Father who sees in secret will reward you*" (Matthew 6:1-4).

My dear friend, whose reward do you want? Do you want God's reward or man's? If you want man's reward, give according to the designs and pressures of the current religious systems that have missed the way of God and are in captivity, and man will reward you. If you want God's reward, give to satisfy the heart of God, irrespective of what men may say or think of you, and your reward will be great in heaven.

Giving and the diversities of ministries

In a normal work of God, the following ministers and ministries would exist. Apostles for the apostolic ministry or planting of churches in new areas, etc; prophets for the prophetic ministry; evangelists for the evangelistic ministry, etc; pastors for the pastoral ministry, teachers for the teaching ministry, etc. There will also be the ministry of healing, helpers, etc. All these ministries must be supported by believers. I am horrified to know that most of the money given to many local churches goes mainly and sometimes only to support the ministry of the resident pastor. What of the apostles who are on the move in the forefront of the battle? What of the prophets, evangelists, teachers, and others whose ministries force them to move from place to place? Must they beg or starve? If you belong to a local assembly where all these ministries and ministers are taken care of, you should give all the money you have for the Lord and His work there, and it will be apportioned out to the different ministers and ministries. If your local church has no vision beyond supplying the needs for the pastor, then you are under no obligation to give all that you have for the Lord there. You should certainly give to the local church but you must also give to support the other ministries and ministers. They are your responsibility before God. Do not only think in terms of your local assembly. Open your eyes and see what is being done to reach others in other parts of the nation or world for the glory of the Lord and support it. If you do not support it, the overall interests of the Lord will be at stake. If there is no work and workers aimed at reaching the whole country, continent, and world for the Lord, then some day the local assembly will also phase out. You do good not only to the other ministers and ministries when you support them, but also you do good to your local assembly. Any pastor who will discourage the support of other ministers and ministries mainly because he wants money for himself or wants authority over much money will come to poverty and judgment.

Giving to the poor

The emphasis today in giving to people in "full-time service" is certainly out of tune with the New Testament. In the early church the emphasis was not on giving to ministers of the gospel, although they did receive support, but on giving to the poor. The ministry of deacons was introduced into the church so that the material needs of the poor might be met on a daily basis (Acts 6: 1). It was not instituted for what it now serves in many a church today that has lost track of the heavenly pattern.

When Paul received his commission from the leaders of the church in Jerusalem he put it this way, "*and when they perceived the grace that was given to me, James and Cephas and John, who were reputed to be pillars, gave to me and Barnabas the right hand of fellowship, that we should go to the Gentiles and they to the circumcised; only they would have us remember the poor, which very thing I was eager to do*" (Galatians 2:9-10). It is all-interesting. They were not told, "Remember the apostles. Remember the elders. Remember this or that programme," but "Remember the poor". The money that was to be collected week after week in the Gentile churches was for the poor (2 Corinthians 8:4; 2 Corinthians 9:1-4). The needs of the poor in the church must be met. Any local church or work that does not have the care-taking of the poor as an important part of her finances has missed the mark! This calls for heart-searching among church leaders and for repentance and action. If your local assembly has no significant room in her budget for the poor, especially those within the church, you have no obligation to give all that you have for the Lord and his work to that assembly. It is also God's work that the needs of the poor are met. If the church would not act collectively, you, as an individual must do something for the poor. If you do not, one day the Lord may say to you, "*Depart from me, you cursed, into the eternal fire prepared for the devil and his angels, for I was hungry and you gave me no food, I was thirsty and you gave me no drink...*" (Matthew 25:41-46). This calls for heart-searching, repentance and the bearing of fruit that befits repentance.

A bank account for God

There is so much confusion in the world and also in many churches about money. No child of God can afford to just become a part of that confusion. If you do not yet know where to invest your money for God and His work, I advise you to start a bank account for God. Put all the money that you have set apart for God into that account so that it will be gaining interest for Him while you sort things out with Him about whom and what to support. When things are sorted out, the money can then be withdrawn and put into the work that He has thus chosen for you to become a part of or to support.

God blessing people with riches

The Bible abounds with examples of people whom the Lord blessed with much wealth. We shall cite just a few. "*And Isaac sowed in that land, and reaped in the same year a hundredfold. The Lord blessed him, and the man became rich and gained more and more until he became very wealthy. He had possessions of flocks and herds and a great household so that the Philistines envied him*" (Genesis 26:12-14). To Solomon the Lord said, "*I give you also what you have not asked, both riches and honour, so that no other king shall compare with you, all your days*" (1 Kings 3:13). About Hezekiah it is said, "*And Hezekiah had very great riches and honour; and he made for himself treasuries for silver, for gold, for precious stones, for spices, for shields, and for all kinds of costly vessels, storehouses also for the yield of grain, wine, and oil and stalls for all kinds of cattle, and sheepfolds. He likewise provided cities for himself, and flocks and herds in abundance, for God had given him very great possessions*" (2 Chronicles 32:27-29). Of Job before his suffering it was said, "*Thou hast blessed the work of his hands, and his possessions have increased in the land*" (Job 1:10). After his suffering the Bible says, "*And the Lord blessed the latter days of Job more than his be-*

ginning; and he had fourteen thousand sheep, six thousand camels, a thousand yoke of oxen, and a thousand she-asses" (Job 42:12). God is still prepared to bless people with wealth in our day.

The dangers of riches

The Lord blesses people with riches so that they may not hoard them. His purposes in making anyone rich is to ensure that that one has much to give to others. There are a number of reasons why the Lord cannot bless someone with wealth so that that person may be selfish. First of all, money has a strong power to imprison its owners and direct their love from the Lord Jesus to the love of it. It competes with God for honour and worship. The Lord Jesus said, "*No one can serve two masters; for either he will hate the one and love the other, or he will be devoted to the one and despise the other. You cannot serve God and mammon*" (Matthew 6:24). The Lord knew what He was saying. He is perfectly correct. He has always been! He further said, "*How hard it will be for those who have riches to enter the kingdom of God!*" (Mark 10:25). The tragic story of the rich young ruler illustrates these truths so clearly. He had nearly all the qualifications that it takes to become a disciple. One thing, however, ruined all his chances. He was too rich. The Lord said to him, "*You lack one thing; go, sell what you have, and give to the poor, and you will have treasure in heaven; and come follow me. At that saying, his countenance fell, and he went away sorrowful, for he had great possessions*" (Mark 10:21-22). This story has been repeated in a million tragic lives that have missed God's best. Is it the tragic story of your life? Do you have inclinations towards the love of money that will make your life story resemble that of the rich young ruler someday?

The Lord Jesus also attributed the lack of spiritual maturity and fruit in many lives to the deceitfulness of riches. He said, "*And others are the ones sown among thorns; they are those who hear the word, but the cares of the world, and the delight in riches and the desire for other things, enter in and choke the word, and it proves unfruitful*" (Mark 4:18-19). If you delight in riches, you will be barren because your heart is thorny.

The apostle Paul continued to teach on the same lines with the Lord. He said, "*There is a great gain in godliness with contentment; for we brought nothing into the world and it is certain we cannot take anything out of the world; but if we have food and clothing, with these we shall be content. But those who desire to be rich fall into temptation, into a snare, into many senseless and hurtful desires that plunge men into ruin and destruction. For the love of money is the root of all evils; it is through this craving that some have wandered away from the faith and pierced their hearts with many pangs*" (1 Timothy 6:6-10).

Do you love money? Do you inwardly crave for the things that it offers? Are you dissatisfied because of money? Do you go worrying about how to make more money? If your answer to these questions is, "yes", you are in great danger. Seek the Lord for deliverance, or you will perish.

There is another reason why no believer can really afford to hoard wealth for himself. The reason is the terrible poverty in the world. Many are dying of starvation or malnutrition. They do not have the basic requirement for contentment food and clothing. In the face of such need all over, how can a disciple of Jesus accumulate wealth for himself? How can he afford to live in luxury while others are starving, and profess to love his neighbour as himself? The apostle John asks, "*If anyone has the world's goods and sees his brother in need, yet closes his heart against him, how does God's love abide in him?*" (1 John 3.17).

Too many believers live in luxury, some in extreme luxury. I write this with pain in my heart, but I am forced nevertheless to write it.

The warning of James which says, "*Come now, you rich, weep and howl for the miseries that are coming upon you. Your riches have rotted and your garments are moth-eaten. Your gold and silver have rusted, and their rust will be evidence against you and will eat your flesh like fire. You have laid up treasure for the last days*" (James 5:1-3). In my travels in many countries both for scientific and for spiritual reasons, I must confess to my utter shame that the most luxury-laden personal house that I have ever stepped foot into belonged to a pastor who professed and preached salvation by faith in the Lord.

Making money for the kingdom

The fact that the love of money is the root of all evil does not mean that believers are not to make money. They should and they must. Money is needed in the treasury of the Lord. We cannot run away from the fact that we need money to live in order to do the business of life.

When the children of Israel left Egypt, they brought out with them a lot of wealth. Although part of it was wasted in building the golden calf, the other part served the useful purpose of building the tabernacle. Had they obeyed the Lord more fully, all of it would have been used in the construction of the tabernacle. We are to use money for eternal profit. The Lord Jesus said, "*And I tell you, make friends for yourselves by means of unrighteous mammon, so that when it fails, they may receive you into the eternal habitations*" (Luke 16:9). Money will fail but the wise disciple would have used it to build treasures in heaven before it fails. I want to recommend that you use all of your abilities to make as much money as you possibly can and, after making it, give it for the work of the Lord and to the poor. In this way you will not be trapped. You will be the winner. However, this calls for a consecration to the Lord that is deep and complete.

There is no room for laziness in the name of spirituality. Do not be lazy out of fear that you will be trapped. Let the Lord reign supremely in your heart and you will have no problem. Laziness and the poverty that results from it are abominations to the Lord. His Word says, "*He who is slack in his work is a brother to him who destroys*" (Proverbs 18:9). "*Hear, my son, and be wise, and direct your mind in the way. Be not among winebibbers, or among gluttonous eaters of meat; for the drunkard and the glutton will come to poverty, and drowsiness will clothe a man with rags*" (Proverbs 23:19-21). The apostle Paul said, "*For you yourselves know how you ought to imitate us; we were not idle when we were with you, we did not eat any one's bread without paying, but with toil and labour we worked night and day that we might not burden any of you. It was not because we have not that right, but to give you in our conduct an example to imitate. For even when we were with you, we gave you this command: if any one will not work, let him not eat. For we hear that some of you are living in idleness, mere busy bodies, not doing any work. Now such persons we command and exhort in the Lord Jesus Christ to do their work in quietness and to earn their own living*" (2 Thessalonians 3:7-12). May every minister imitate Paul's example! May every believer do the same!

So all believers must work hard. They must make the largest sums of money that they possibly can make, but they must give these away and they will have treasures in heaven.

Owning nothing, yet having everything

When a believer makes a lot of money and gives it away, he will in a sense own nothing. This is good; for that is the true spirit of a Levite. The Bible says, "*At that time the Lord set apart the tribe of Levi to carry the ark of the covenant of the Lord, to stand before the Lord to minister to him and to bless in his name to this day. Therefore, Levi has no portion or inheritance with his brothers. The Lord is his inheritance, as the Lord your God said to him*" (Deuteronomy 10:8-9). Earlier on, the Lord had said to Aaron, "*You shall have no inheritance in their land, neither shall you have any portion among them, I am your portion and your inheritance among the people of Israel*" (Numbers 18:20). The Lord asked that the Levites should have no portion. He gave them Himself as their portion; as their inheritance and, by doing so, he gave them everything. They owned nothing, yet he gave them everything because He has everything. Because they possessed nothing, they could not develop possessive attitudes about the things He gave them. They just held them for Him. They kept these things for the Lord and used them for the Lord. They had all the tithes to use and the cities to live in, but it was always with the understanding that these things were the Lord's.

The Levites were the priests in the Old Testament. True believers are priests in the New Testament (1 Peter 2:5; Revelation 1:6). They, too, like Levites must own nothing. They must have God as their only Possession and, in having God alone, they have everything. The apostle Paul could say of himself as "*having nothing, and yet possessing everything*" (2 Corinthians 6:10). Why was this so? It was so because although he owned nothing he had God and, therefore, had everything and thus having everything, he was able to make many rich. He was able then to be in a state of constant contentment. He said: "*Not that 1 complain of want; for I have learned, in whatever state I am, to be content. I know how to be abased, and I know how to abound; in any and all circumstances I have learned the secret of facing plenty and hunger, abundance and want. I can do all things in Him who strengthens me*" (Philippians 4:11-13).

How could he be content in all circumstances? It is because he owned nothing, yet everything. God was his Possession; his Inheritance. May we, too, you and I, experience that as our normal way of life!

Selling all

The rich young ruler's heart was welded to his possessions. If his heart was to be given to Jesus, it had to be liberated. Jesus suggested the remedy for this liberation, but because the price was too much, he went away sadly because he had great possessions. There is a sense in which Jesus asks everyone who would come after Him to sell all. The principle is the same a renunciation of wealth and a possession of God. The practical implication may differ but they may be manifested in our lives as it was in the life of an Englishman. He was earning fifty pounds per month out of which he gave ten pounds each month to the Lord and his work. After some time, his position changed and his salary doubled. He now earned one hundred pounds each month. He did not increase his expenditure. He continued as usual to live on forty pounds a month and this time gave sixty pounds to the Lord and His work. In his own way he "sold" all. The example of an American businessman also illustrates the total detachment from things. When he just started his business, he gave God ten percent of his income and lived on 90 percent. The following year, the Lord blessed him more and he gave Him 20 percent and lived on 80 percent. This continued until at the height of it he was giving the Lord 90 percent of his income and living on 10 percent. He had learned the secret of growing rich by giving to the Lord. May we go and do likewise. Are your possessions standing between you and God's best for your life? Go and sell them and give them to the poor and you will have riches in heaven and come, follow the Lord. He said, "*So, therefore, whoever of you does not renounce all that he has cannot be my disciple*" (Luke 4:33). Have you renounced all? Are you placing all that you have at His disposal? If not, you are not a disciple.

The love that constrains

A whole-hearted commitment to the Lord Jesus, to live a life of self-denial and poverty, not to love the world, can only be done out of love for the Lord Jesus. It has to be His love wooing, leading, constraining us into action. The Bible says, "*The love of Christ constrains us*" (2 Corinthians 5:14). A million sermons may not change a man's heart, but one real look at the face of the Lord Jesus will do it. Look at His bleeding side. Look at His nail-pierced hands. Look at His crown of thorns and hear Him say to you, "I suffered all these because I love you. Won't you respond to that love?" Please, look at Him again, who, though rich, for your sake became poor as He hung on the cross. Is it right to offer a lesser sacrifice than your all when He gave you His all?

Even if for some reason the love of the Lord for you did not touch you, does the cry of sinners without Christ not touch you? Listen, sinners in their billions are facing the grim possibility of an eternity without Christ. Soon they may be in eternal fire and their cry will go up forever. Part of that cry will be because you did not care. If you offered your all, many of them would be in heaven. Would you be content to spend happy years in heaven with the blood of lost sinners on you? Do you not care? Does a love for them not force you to do all that you can for them? Think soberly about these things and do not rest until God has told you what you must do.

We build here with what you send from the world

The story is told of two women who knew the Lord Jesus in a personal way. One was very rich and the other one was her house servant. The housemaid sacrificed her being, property, and all on the Lord and in His service. The rich woman gave some of her enormous wealth to the Lord and His work, but retained enough and went on to live luxuriously. Later on both of them died and, as true believers, they went to heaven. The Lord Jesus asked one of His servants to show them their heavenly homes. The one who was the housemaid was placed in a super deluxe mansion which was beautiful and grandiose beyond any human imagination. The one who was the mistress was given another house, very beautiful and wonderful, the product of the Master's own work (all mansions in heaven are the Lord's personal production) but in every way it was inferior to the one that was given to the woman who was her housemaid on earth. She thought that a mistake had been made and so complained, saying, that the bigger and better house should be hers and the smaller one should be that of her housegirl. She was told that there was no mistake for "in heaven there are no mistakes and no houseservants" and "we build here with what you send from the world." It was not the quantity, the degree of gift that mattered to the Lord. It was the quality, the degree of sacrifice involved that made the difference. What mattered was what was left behind after a gift was made to Him and in that the houseservant made far more progress than the mistress and won a heavenly treasure which she would keep through all eternity. In terms of the quality and quantity of your gifts, what type of heavenly home is being built for you?

The consequences of not giving to the lord

Can a believer refuse to give to the Lord or can he give sparingly and bear no consequences for such sin? The emphatic answer from the word of God is No! There are serious consequences for not giving.

The first consequence is that you will not be given spiritual riches. Not giving to the Lord is dishonesty. It is unfaithfulness over things that must soon pass away. The Lord said, "*He who is faithful in a very little way is faithful also in much; and he who is dishonest in a very little way is dishonest also in much. If then you have not been faithful in the unrighteous mammon, who will entrust to you the true riches? And if you have not been faithful in that which is another's, who will give you that which is your own?*" (Luke 16:10-12). Our possessions really belong to the Lord. They are also passing wealth. The Lord has given them to us to find out if we can handle them without greed for Him. If we do not give them back to Him, we are testifying to the fact that we are not fit to be entrusted with the treasures of the Kingdom, and God will ensure that we do not have any!

The second consequence is that what we keep back will not be a blessing to us. The Lord once said, "Is it a time for you yourselves to dwell in your panelled houses, while this house lies in ruins? Now, therefore, thus says the Lord of hosts: Consider how you have fared. You have sown much, and harvested little; you eat, but never have enough; you drink, but you never have your fill; clothe yourselves, but no one is warm; and he who earns wages earns wages to put them into a bag with holes." Thus says the Lord of hosts: "Consider how you have fared. Go up to the hills and bring wood and build the house, that I may take pleasure in it and that I may appear in my glory, says the Lord. You have looked for much, and, Io, it came to little; and when you brought it home, I blew it away. Why? says the Lord of hosts. Because of my house that lies in ruins, while you busy yourselves each with his own house. Therefore, the heavens above you have withdrawn the dew, and the earth has withheld its produce. And I have called for a drought upon the land and the hills, upon the grain, the new wine, the oil, upon what the ground brings forth, upon man and cattle, and upon all their labours" (Haggai 1:4-11). The Lord says the same thing today. When believers fail to give to the Lord, the Lord will inflict the land with drought, etc. Does that explain the increasing number of droughts and floods the world over? Does that explain the diminishing resources of many of God's children? Does that explain why your salary increases but you are overwhelmed by needs? Is it because you do not give sufficiently to the Lord and, therefore, He has put a hole in your economic system? Nothing will work until you repent and give the Lord what is His.

The third consequence is that you, being a thief from God, are cursed with a curse. The Lord said, "*Will man rob God? Yet you are robbing me. But you say, 'How are we robbing thee?' In your tithes and offerings. You are cursed with a curse, for you are robbing me; the whole nation of you*" (Malachi 3:8-9). A person who does not give sacrificially to the Lord is a thief. It is not permitted that a man should steal from another man but what if a man decides to steal from God? He is cursed with a curse for robbing God. Are you like that? Are you under a curse because you have been robbing God? imagine you, a believer, but a thief from God! How horrible!

When God curses people, they can no longer make spiritual progress. They cannot receive revelation from the Lord and they become barren in many ways. The spiritual malady of many of God's children may be traced to the fact that they are thieves from God. There is, however, a way out of the curse repentance and restitution. The thief does not only stop stealing, he returns all that he has stolen before. You thief from God, go and do the same and the curse will be lifted.

Only believers should give for god's work

Although there are financial needs of God's work, God will not receive money from unbelievers. If a person hears the Gospel of the Lord Jesus and refuses to give his life over to the Lord Jesus, such a person becomes a mocker, nay, an enemy of God and, as such, can never contribute to the building of the kingdom of God until his spiritual condition has changed.

To begin with, believers whose lives are not right with God offend God by giving to Him. What they offer is not accepted by the Lord. Men may use it, but God will have nothing to do with it. In talking to Israel who had sinned, God said, "*I hate, I despise your feasts, and I take no delight in your solemn assemblies. Even though you offer me your burnt offerings and cereal offerings, I will not accept them, and the peace offerings of your fatted beasts I will not look upon. Take away from me the noise of your songs; to the melody of your harps I will not listen*" (Amos 5:21-23). If God would not accept the gifts of His children who have sinned, how less would He regard the gifts of those who, by rejecting His Son, team up with His enemy? He will surely have nothing to do with them and with their gifts.

The Bible says, "*The sacrifice of the wicked is an abomination to the Lord*" (Proverbs 15:8). The sacrifice of an unbeliever is an abomination to the Lord. Anyone who receives gifts from unbelievers in the name of the Lord receives abominations and will himself share in the judgment to be levied on the abominable.

The Bible further says, "*The sacrifice of the wicked is an abomi-nation; how much more when he brings it with an evil intent!*" (Prov-erbs 21:27). Even when a wicked person (all unbelievers who have heard the gospel and rejected Christ are wicked) offers a sacrifice with a good intent, it is nevertheless an abomination. It is worse when he brings it with an evil intent!

There are many reasons why unbelievers give. It may be that by giving they escape from paying taxes which are almost as high as the money itself. In such cases, God is just being used to obtain a good name. Is it right that the enemies of God should be allowed to use the Lord to advertise themselves? Unbelievers may also give to quieten their consciences over sins committed. Is it right for a believer to encourage or help an unbeliever to ease his conscience instead of facing the reality of his sin, confessing it, and turning to the Lord?

Can God accept a man's gifts when the man himself has, by rebellion, turned his back to the Lord Jesus? Is it not cheating to encourage a man to give for some religious purpose in full knowledge that God has no hand in that gift? Where is Christian honesty? Where is Christian integrity? Must money-loving ministers be allowed to use God's name to enrich themselves or their pet interests or "ministries?".

The Bible says, "*Beloved, it is a loyal thing you do when you render any service to the brethren, especially to strangers, who have testified to your love before the Church. You will do well to send them on their journey as befits God's service. For they have set out for his sake and have accepted nothing from the heathen. So we ought to support such men that we may be fellow-workers in the truth*" (3 John 5-8). These heathens from whom the ministers of the gospel in the early Church would not accept gifts still exist today. They are not only found in the unevangelized lands. They are also found in America, Europe, "Christianised" towns in Africa, etc and, because they have heard the gospel but rejected God's only Son and yet continue to play religious games, their judgment shall be more terrible. Their gifts are also twice as abominable as the gifts of those who have never heard the gospel. Those who canvass for money from them for the work of the Kingdom shall share their abominations.

Dear reader, if you have not personally received the Lord Jesus as your Lord and Saviour, do not give to the Lord or His work. Your gift is an abomination and those who receive it deceive you. You will remain condemned before God until you repent and receive Jesus, even if you were to give your whole fortune away.

The Investment of Life

We have been looking at the investment of money for the building of the Kingdom of the Lord. This is wholesome and good, but there is also the investment of life. You have just one life. You could waste it or you could invest it for God. Your lifespan too is short. If you are thirty years old, then you have just about forty years to go and it will be over (should you live to be three score and ten and should the Lord Jesus delay His return). What will you do?

Many careers are before you. You could become a statesman or a scientist or any such thing. These are all very good. However, could it be that the Lord is calling you to serve Him directly in the Gospel enterprise? Could it be that He is calling you to be one of the lonely young men who will go to a lonely village on an isolated mountain top to tell them of His love? Will you sacrifice your career, fame, honour, and reputation for Him?

Our Head of State has many young men offering to serve him all the time in one area of government or the other. But what of the Lord of glory? Many offer to go and preach the gospel. Too many offer who are not qualified. Some offer because they want a way of earning a living and preaching is the only one open to them. This is most sad when mediocre workers fill the service that ought to have the best people in the whole world. Where are the well-trained doctors of philosophy, masters of arts, etc, who could make a real success in the world who are giving up these lesser pursuits for the one high pursuit of serving Jesus and serving Him only?

Will you turn your back to the world and "waste" your life on Jesus? A young intelligent man at twenty-one years was at the top of the list of those admitted into the university. He turned it down and said, "I want to serve the Lord Jesus. I have no other ambition." He went ahead and preached the gospel without salary or anything else as guarantee from man. Where are his counterparts today?

When will men of God give up their positions in administration, industry, education, etc, that the prior claims of the Lord might be met? If the Lord has called you to such service and, out of a love for the world, you stay at a cherished profession and give Him the large sums of money that you make there, His heart will remain unfulfilled. Your gifts will stink before Him and your sacrifices will remain totally unacceptable; for did he not say that obedience was better than sacrifice?

If the Lord has called you to so serve Him, is it right to postpone it until some time in the future when circumstances will be more favourable? Is it right to wait until your life is wasted on secondary pursuits and then to come toward the end of your life to make God a rubbish heap by dumping on Him the scarred remains of a wasted life? Does He not want you now? Be careful and act wisely.

I command you in the name of the Lord Jesus that you should take time before God after reading this article to settle the prior claim of the Lord and the Kingdom on you. Do not do anything else for Him until He has told you what you must do.

Too late

For those who truly love the Lord Jesus and who have Him as their only love; for those who with the Psalmist can say, "*Whom have I in heaven but thee?*" (Psalm 73:25), I want to say that it is too late to dream about another promotion from men, too late to dream about buying a car or changing the smaller one for a bigger and more luxurious one. It is too late to dream about a bigger salary, more honour from men and women. It is too late to plan how to please the world, how to fit comfortably in it. It is too late to dream about a bigger house, newer clothes, more shoes. It is too late to compromise for the sake of peace.

It is time for one thing and one thing only. It is time to love Jesus supremely and time to take up your cross and follow Him and, like Him, be crucified to self, the world, and all else. It is time to take the Gospel to the ends of the world and to preach it powerfully and biblically; so that it will cause you your life and your all.

It is time to put all the money you have into the business of the Gospel and let it be used while the doors are open. Do not store it up in a will. Let it be used now.

The existentialist god: A time for action

There is a sense in which God is an Existentialist. He is critically concerned with the here and the now. He says, "Go and work for me today." Today, if you hear His Voice do not harden your heart. The financial needs of God's work in this and other countries are urgent matters that cannot be postponed. If you have been robbing Him of what is His, then today is the day to repent and bear fruit that befits repentance.

Do you hear His voice saying to you, "Go and work for me today"? For whom are you working now? Do you hear Him? He says, "You, go and work for me (for the Lord of glory) today." He means it when He says today. You would do well to obey.

My beloved friend, for the sake of the Lord, for the sake of His coming Kingdom, for the sake of His Church which must be built to maturity, for the sake of the glorious gospel which must be proclaimed before the doors are closed, I invite you to enter into a covenant of love with Jesus beginning from now and give Him your all in a practical sense; for "if any man loves the world, the love of the Father is not in him."

Practical action you should think about and act upon today

There are a number of things that you can do to bank in heaven.

Read them and do not rest until you have done something about it.

1. Have you savings in the bank? Are you sure the Lord has asked you to save that money? Is the money really safe? What of thieves like inflation and the like? Have you carefully examined the fact that all money that is kept in an earthly bank is not sure to always belong to you? Have you prayerfully faced the following words of Jesus, "*Do not lay up for yourselves treasures on earth, where moth and rust consume and where thieves break in and steal, but lay up for yourselves treasures in heaven, where neither moth nor rust consumes and where thieves do not break in and steal. For where your treasure is, there will your heart be also*" (Matthew 6:19-22)?

What you have in the bank is not really yours. It could become the property of another any time. Your only savings is the money which you have already sent to the bank of heaven by investment in the Lord and His service. Monies that are not already transferred to heaven may never be transferred. The future is all uncertain. If you are wise, act now! Is it right that you stock money in a bank account to guarantee your future needs while people are perishing? Why should you not close your bank account and invest the contents into the work of the Lord today? Can you not count on the Lord to supply your needs in the future? Can you not count on the Lord to supply the needs of your wife and children in the future? Is your saving account a better security for the future than the Lord?

2. Have you investments on earth? Have you houses, lands, farms, etc? Have you carefully and sincerely prayed about the possibility of selling, some or all of them and banking the money in hea-

ven now by investing in God's work?

3. Are you living in a luxurious house? The Son of Man had no place to lay His head. Have you prayed about the possibility of moving to a cheaper house and thereby increasing your investment in the Kingdom of God? A thousand years from now it will not matter if you lived in a mansion or in a hut. However, it will matter how much you had in your heavenly account.

4. Do you have any jewellery? Sell it and transfer the money into your heavenly account by putting it into God's work. Do you have anything that you do not really need? Give it to the poor or sell it and invest the money into the work of the gospel.

5. Look at your budget. Can you reduce the amount that is spent on some items and thereby increase your giving to the Lord's work? Are there no items on it that should be scrapped completely? A communist said the following, "We live in virtual poverty. We turn back to the party every penny we make above what is absolutely necessary to keep us alive." Have you even considered the fact that you may not be able to win the communist because his consecration to communism is greater than yours to Christ? Unless you too can say, "I live in virtual poverty. I invest in the work of the gospel every penny I make above what is absolutely necessary to keep me alive," you are perhaps a hypocrite. You are infatuated with the world. You have no message for the communist.

6. Do not say that you are living a sacrificial life when things like soft drinks, coffee, tea, etc, adorn your table. You can live a perfectly healthy life, in fact, a healthier life without any of them. You can live without very many of the things you have. If the gospel has not cut down your expenditures, you may still be in the old life.

7. It is a sin to pray for anything that is a luxury. A luxury is

anything that you do not need to keep you alive and enable you to get the gospel to the lost.

8. If you are a disciple, you need to think carefully as to why you should possess the things that the Lord Jesus and the early apostles did not possess or bother about. You need to ask yourself, "Am I learning to live as simply as Jesus and the apostles lived? Where is there luxury? Where is there worldliness? What must I do about it now?"

9. The Lord Jesus said, "He who is faithful in a very little way is faithful also in much; and he who is dishonest in a very little way is dishonest also in much" (Luke 16: 10). Are you faithful in giving to the Lord out of your small income? How much did you give last year? How much did you give last month? How much will you give at the end of this month? It is necessary to write down the actual figures and look at them in the face. Do not read further until you have actually written out what you gave last year, last month, and the project for giving this month.

10. The apostle John wrote, "*Do not love the world or the things in the world. If any one loves the world, love for the Father is not in him. For all that is in the world, the lust of the flesh and the lust of the eyes and the pride of life, is not of the Father but of the world. And the world passes away, and the lust of it; but he who does the will of God abides forever*" (1 John 2:15-17).

Do you love the world?

Do you love the things that are in the world?

If you do, then you can be sure that love for the Father is not in you.

11. The apostle Paul wrote, "*There is great gain in godliness with contentment, for we brought nothing into the world, and we cannot take anything out of the world; but if we have food and clothing, with these we shall be content. But those who desire to be rich fall into temptation, into a snare, into many senseless and hurtful desires that plunge men into ruin and destruction. For the love of money is the root of all evils; it is through this craving that some have wandered away from the faith and pierced their hearts with many pangs*" (1 Timothy 6:6-10).

Are you contented with what you have? Discontent is sin. Perpetual discontent is perpetual sin. Are you thereby living in perpetual sin? How can you have fellowship with the Lord Jesus while living in perpetual sin? Are you craving for more money and more things? Repent and transfer what you have now into your heavenly account. Do it at once. Do not be deceived. Ask the Lord to show you the true condition of your heart.

12. Do you desire what others have? That is covetousness. Do you desire more and more things? Are you keeping what you do not actually need? That is greed. The covetous will not inherit the Kingdom of God. The one way out of covetousness is to repent and radically invest your all in the Kingdom of God. Do it now and continue to do it.

13. Your treasure is either on earth or in heaven.

Your heart is where your treasure is.

Your heart is, therefore, either in heaven or on earth.

Where is it?

14. Jesus banked in heaven.

The apostles banked in heaven.

All consecrated Christians bank in heaven.

Go and do likewise.

15. Begin to bank in heaven today.

Continue to bank in heaven in an increasing way.

Grow in banking in heaven until you finally have nothing on earth because all has been banked in heaven.

Very important

If you have not yet received Jesus as your Lord and Saviour, I encourage you to receive Him. Here are some steps to help you,

ADMIT that you are a sinner by nature and by practice and that on your own you are without hope. Tell God you have personally sinned against Him in your thoughts, words and deeds. Confess your sins to Him, one after another in a sincere prayer. Do not leave out any sins that you can remember. Truly turn from your sinful ways and abandon them. If you stole, steal no more. If you have been committing adultery or fornication, stop it. God will not forgive you if you have no desire to stop sinning in all areas of your life, but if you are sincere, He will give you the power to stop sinning.

BELIEVE that Jesus Christ, who is God's Son, is the only Way, the only Truth and the only Life. Jesus said, "*I am the way, the truth and the life; no one comes to the Father, but by me*" (John 14:6). The Bible says, "*For there is one God, and there is one mediator between God and men, the man Christ Jesus, who gave himself as a ransom for all*" (1 Timothy 2:5-6). "*And there is salvation in no one else (apart from Jesus), for there is no other name under heaven given among men by which we must be saved*" (Acts 4:12). "*But to all who received him, who believed in his name, he gave power to become children of God...*" (John 1:12). BUT,

CONSIDER the cost of following Him. Jesus said that all who follow Him must deny themselves, and this includes selfish financial, social and other interests. He also wants His followers to take up their crosses and follow Him. Are you prepared to abandon your own interests daily for those of Christ? Are you prepared to be led in a new direction by Him? Are you prepared to suffer for Him and die for Him if need be? Jesus will have nothing to do with half-hearted people. His demands are total. He will only receive and forgive those who are prepared to follow Him AT ANY COST. Think about it and count the cost. If you are prepared to follow Him, come what may, then there is something to do.

INVITE Jesus to come into your heart and life. He says, "*Behold I stand at the door and knock. If anyone hears my voice and opens the door (to his heart and life), I will come in to him and eat with him, and he with me* " (Revelation 3:20). Why don't you pray a prayer like the following one or one of your own construction as the Holy Spirit leads ?

"Lord Jesus, I am a wretched, lost sinner who has sinned in thought, word and deed. Forgive all my sins and cleanse me. Receive me, Saviour and transform me into a child of God. Come into my heart now and give me eternal life right now. I will follow you at all costs, trusting the Holy Spirit to give me all the power I need."

When you pray this prayer sincerely, Jesus answers at once and justifies you before God and makes you His child.

Please write to me and I will pray for you and help you as you go on with Jesus Christ...

If you have received the Lord Jesus-Christ after reading this book, please write to us at the following addresse :

For Europe :

Editions du Livre Chrétien

4, Rue du Révérend Père Cloarec

92400 Courbevoie

Courriel : editionlivrechretien@gmail.com

ABOUT THE AUTHOR